EAGLE ON ICE

Lone Adélie penguin (courtesy Wendell Wilson Collection).

EAGLE ON ICE

Eagle Scout Paul Siple's Antarctic
Adventures with Commander Byrd

Patricia Potter Wilson
and Roger Leslie

VANTAGE PRESS
New York

May 2009

Contents

Acknowledgments

This remarkable story focuses on the 1928–1930 adventures of nineteen-year-old Paul Siple, the Eagle Scout selected to go on Commander Richard E. Byrd's first expedition to Antarctica. Although it is a book written for middle school students, the authors believe that *Eagle on Ice* will be of interest to all ages.

Without the input of the persons we consulted during this project, *Eagle on Ice* would not have been possible. The "persons consulted" listed in the Appendices of this book provided the authors with a wonderful insight into the time period in which this grand adventure is set as well as the hardships of survival on this beautiful, unrelenting continent. As the story is read, it is important to realize that the setting for much of the story, "Little America," broke off from the Antarctic continent in 1987 and eventually sank to the bottom of the Southern Ocean at an unrecorded location.

Quotes from diaries, newspaper and magazine articles, and other resources are used throughout this book to provide readers with a flavor of the language during this exciting period of history. References for these quotes are provided in the Appendices.

Much credit for this book goes to Paul Siple's wife, Ruth, who shared a wealth of information about Paul and his early years. At the beginning of the project Ruth suggested the title *Eagle on Ice*. Ruth passed away recently, but her memories of Paul helped mold this work.

Jane Siple DeWitt, Paul's daughter, was also a significant contributor to this book.

We are also grateful to our colleagues—Melissa Mares, Dr. Richard Abrahamson, Dr. Barbara Samuels, and Dr. Maureen White—who provided advice and support throughout the writing of this book. Members of the Antarctican Society such as Dr. Paul Dalrymple, Dr. Richard Chappell, and John Splettstoesser were also instrumental in the development of *Eagle on Ice*.

The illustrations, both photographs and drawings, play an important role in helping readers to better understand what it was like to live in Antarctica in 1928–1930. They also provide readers with a sense of the many adventures that young Paul Siple encountered. Illustrator Laura Moore Brown, a former New York City District Attorney and television legal commentator, created the maps of Antarctica and Little America as well as the delightful penguins that adorn the Appendices.

Photographs from the First Byrd Antarctic Expedition were found after endless hours of searching the Byrd Polar Research Center Archives at The Ohio State University Libraries and the National Archives in College Park, Maryland. The most precious of the photographs, the personal ones of Paul as a young man, are from the Paul Siple Family collection. The more recent photographs of the wildlife and landscapes of Antarctica were generously shared by Captain Wendell Wilson, a retired international captain for Delta Air Lines who has traveled and photographed the world for over forty years.

EAGLE ON ICE

Prologue: The Will to Survive

Little America, Antarctica
Fall 1929

The Antarctic winds howled and whipped, flinging ice and snow into Paul's eyes as the storm raged around him. His eyelashes quickly stuck together as the frozen crystals clung tightly. No landmarks were visible, only a milky scene of sameness spread out before him. The dangerous blizzard was announcing its arrival, and the worst was yet to come.

Despite the gusting winds and bitter, bone-chilling cold, he felt and heard nothing but his own heartbeat pounding as the blood coursed through his veins, echoing in his ears with a whooshing sound. He turned his head side to side, his neck chafing against the stiff, frozen collar of his parka. Squinting hard beneath heavily frozen lashes, his eyes searched for the horizon, seeking something familiar, anything. All he could see was a blank canvas of nothingness in every direction. Nineteen-year-old Paul struggled to maintain his composure and had a fleeting thought of his family and friends, secure and warm thousands of miles away back home in Erie, Pennsylvania. The moment passed in an instant as Paul willed himself not to give in to panic. He had to remain calm.

His merit badge training and natural instinct is all that would separate him from certain death. Commander

Byrd and the men back in Little America were counting on him. He knew what he had to do. Taking in a deep breath, Paul took a step to the side, moving carefully and checking the firmness of the snow beneath his feet. His throat seared from the frigid air. He took another step in the opposite direction, cautiously feeling his way for any subtle change. He had to survive—he was an Eagle Scout—an "Eagle on Ice."

One

From Scout to Explorer

America
Spring/Summer 1928

Byrd's News-making Plans

Growing up in Erie, Pennsylvania in the early 1900s, Paul Siple could best be described by his parents, friends, and teachers as a curious, determined, self-motivated boy who thrived on learning about the world around him. An inquisitive youngster, Paul always enjoyed exploring the outdoors. He would watch insects, animals, and study each plant from root to bud. As he grew older and even more interested, he began investigating the nearby woods, trekking through area swamps, and dreaming of real adventure. Paul, with an ever-present thirst for knowledge, was always the boy wanting to know how nature worked, and why.

In 1920, at age twelve, he joined Boy Scout Troop Number 24, a perfect place to satisfy his curiosity and desire to learn. This decision would prove to be a life-altering event that would forever shape his future. There among his fellow troop members, and under the guidance

Eagle Scout Paul Siple (courtesy Siple Family Collection).

of his trusted scout leaders, Paul developed a hunger and passion for science and discovery. Paul's curiosity and profound determination led him to earn an impressive fifty-nine merit badges, achieving the distinction of Eagle Scout at the early age of fifteen.

Through the newspapers and radio Paul constantly kept up with the adventures of his hero, world famous explorer Commander Richard Byrd. In 1926 Byrd became the first person to fly over the North Pole. Two years later, Byrd set out in pursuit of another world record, leading a polar expedition, but this time taking off from the Antarctic continent. If successful, he would become the first person to fly over the South Pole and explore a vast and previously unseen area.

Byrd's proposed expedition ignited a fever of excitement across the nation as newspapers tracked and eagerly reported each stage of the planning process. This event was a huge undertaking and Americans were fascinated with the prospect of an adventure in a remote area so few people had ever seen. The South Pole had only previously been visited twice before by two other small expeditions, and no airplane had ever attempted to fly over the region. Byrd would be the first, and if successful, aerial photographs of the terrain taken during his flyover would provide an unprecedented look at the Pole's unique geography. The public was captivated, as was Paul. Aviation technology at the time was not advanced enough to sustain a flight to the Pole from New Zealand or Australia because of the great distance. Byrd devised a risky plan that involved a plane on skis that would take off from his expedition base for the Pole, a feat never attempted.

Adding to the allure, this historic journey would utilize new technologies and innovations unlike any other prior expeditions. Previous explorers, such as Norwegian explorer Roald Amundsen and four daring men, made the long treacherous journey from their Framheim base camp in the Bay of Whales to the South Pole by dog sledges on December 14, 1911. They were successful, managing to return safely to their base camp without incident, but news of their achievement didn't reach home until they returned by sailing ships much later. British explorer Captain Robert Scott reached the Pole on January 17, 1912, but unfortunately he and his four companions perished on the return due to severe weather conditions and inadequate food supplies. Without the aid of outside communications, their plight was not discovered until it was too late to save them. For the first time in history, Byrd and his fellow explorers would have radio and telegraph contact with the rest of the world, as well as within their own exploring parties.

When the list of expedition jobs was revealed, thousands of men submitted their applications as volunteers hoping to participate in this far-flung journey. They began competing for the coveted positions that would ultimately lead them to Antarctica under Byrd's command. The adventure was officially underway.

Expedition Job Opportunities

Aerial photographer
Airplane mechanics
Airplane navigator
Carpenters
Chief cook
Cook helpers
Dog drivers
Geologist
Machinists
Mechanics
Meteorologist
Moviemaker
Newspaper reporter
Physician
Physicist
Pilots
Radio operators
Sailmaker
Scientists
Ski experts
Supply officers
Surveyors
Tailor
Taxidermist
Wood craftsmen

Nuts, Bolts and Planes

Byrd understood the financial demands of such an undertaking and sought public donations to fund the expedition. Corporations such as Ford (best known for transportation), Maxwell House (best known for coffee), and Beechnut (best known for chewing gum) donated large amounts of their products. Companies and organizations such as the Todd Ship Yard, the Rogers Brothers Seed Company, and the National Geographic Society donated other gifts.

In an era when the public received the majority of their news through local newspapers, and the events reported had occurred a day or more before, the media planned to provide Americans with information on the events almost as soon as they happened. In an unprecedented move to capture every moment, *The New York Times* would be sending reporter Russell Owen on the expedition to record the news in Antarctica and to send radio dispatches back to New York. Not to be outdone, Hollywood's Paramount Pictures donated a team of two movie men, Joe Rucker and Willard Van der Veer, to document the heroic expedition through motion pictures and photographs. On their return to America, newsreels would be distributed to the theaters around the world.

Estimated costs of the Antarctic trip steadily rose to over a half-million dollars, a staggering sum in 1928. In an attempt to contain costs, Byrd bought and refurbished two old supply ships for the journey. In addition to the supply ships, two large Norwegian whaling ships volunteered to help transport the explorers to Antarctica.

To increase the geographical area they could explore, Byrd secured two small single engine aircraft: a Fokker Universal called the *Virginia* and a Fairchild with folding wings named *Stars and Stripes*. For his long historic South Pole flight he purchased a large Ford trimotor plane, christened the *Floyd Bennett*. Bennett, a very close friend of Byrd's, accompanied him on the historic North Pole flight in 1926, but soon after he died of pneumonia while on a rescue mission for a downed German airship in Newfoundland. Byrd was saddened to lose his friend and fellow explorer, and naming the plane in Bennett's memory was a way to honor their friendship.

Large quantities of supplies would prove critical for an exploration of this magnitude. Byrd commented in his journal, "In their holds and on their cluttered decks are over 500 tons of supplies and material; there are at least 5,000 different kinds of things, ranging from thumb tacks to airplanes; and every single thing is essential, in one way or another, to our unrelieved stay in the Antarctic."

A Sampling of Expedition Supplies

Food
4,000 pounds of Pork Loin
1,500 pounds of Calf Liver (for vitamins)
1,000 pounds each of Hot Dogs, Cigarettes and Pipe Tobacco
500 pounds of Chewing Gum
10 tons of Sugar
5 tons each of Beef and Flour
3 tons of Bacon
2 tons each of Smoked Ham and Corn Beef
1 ton each of fresh Hams, Veal and Dried Milk
1/2 ton of Lamb and Mutton
3,500 Chickens
2,500 Turkeys
40 tons of Dog Biscuits

Medical Supplies
200 Packages of Tetanus Antitoxin
450 pounds of Ether (anesthetic)
"Other Liquor" (described as *for medicinal purposes only*)
Seasickness Remedies
Dressings, Sutures

Clothing
Special Footwear including Skis and Snowshoes

Equipment
Radio Equipment, Scientific Instruments and Mechanical Tools
3 Airplanes (disassembled and crated for the long journey)
Early Model Snowmobile
1 large Drum of Alcohol for Developing Photos

Miscellaneous
15 Harmonicas
12 Ukeleles
6 Guitars
1 Electrical Player Piano
3,000 Books

When Byrd announced his plan to take one teen explorer on the expedition, he immediately caught the attention of America's youth. Headlines in *The New York Times* on August 13, 1928 read: "SCOUTS IN RACE FOR HONOR OF JOINING BYRD'S EXPEDITION." Byrd extended his offer exclusively to the members of the Boy Scouts of America. The criteria required applicants to be between the ages of seventeen and twenty and members in good standing with the Boy Scouts of America for at least two years. Applicants must have attained the rank of First Class Scout or Able Sea Scout. Preference would be given to scouts with merit badges in areas directly relating to the needs of the polar expedition including astronomy, taxidermy, hiking, carpentry, photography, signaling, and surveying. Experience in boating and camping, particularly winter camping, was also required. Each applicant was expected to complete a 500–1000 word essay stating the reasons why he wishes to become a member of this expedition and why he feels he is qualified.

As a nineteen-year-old Eagle Scout, Paul met the stringent criteria with flying colors. Exhilarated by the challenge and inspired by the chance to meet his hero, Paul was eager to be part of this historic expedition to the continent of ice but knew the competition would be tough. If he got selected, it would mean an eighteen-month interruption in his education at Allegheny College, but Paul knew this once in a lifetime opportunity would be worth putting his studies on hold.

The Competition

Thousands of scouts yearning for adventure joined Paul by applying for the chance to be selected for the historic Antarctic expedition. But the competition was much more difficult than even Paul could imagine. In one section of the application the scouts were asked to explain their reasons for applying and to list their specific qualifications. Paul's impressive fifty-nine merit badges far exceeded the twenty-one required to become an Eagle Scout, and many of his merit badges did relate directly to the needs of the expedition, including badges in camping, seamanship, and taxidermy. Despite his superior qualifications, Paul was apprehensive about the selection process. He wanted this opportunity more than he had ever wanted anything else and hoped the committee would reward his resolve.

Paul Siple's Scout Badges
Related to the Needs of the Expedition

Astronomy
Bird Study
Botany Conservation
Camping
Carpentry
Cooking
Firemanship
First Aid
Forestry
Insect Life
Machinery
Personal Health
Photography
Pioneering
Reptile Study
Safety
Seamanship
Signaling (communication)
Surveying
Taxidermy
Weather
Zoology

At the beginning of the rigorous selection process officials of the local scout councils studied the thousands of applications. After narrowing the applicants down to eighty-eight they made their recommendations to National Office. The committee members at this level carefully and impartially examined each of the candidate's papers. They found the essay on "scout's reason for applying" proved to clearly set the boys apart from one another. Eventually, six finalists emerged and were invited to appear before the committee at the Boy Scout headquarters in New York City. They arrived on August 9, 1928, for the final stage of competition. The scouts competed over a period of ten grueling days, participating in complex skill challenges, the Army Alpha Intelligence Test, personal interviews, and undergoing comprehensive physical exams.

Boy Scout Finalists
Commander Byrd's Expedition

Donald H. Cooper	Tacoma, Washington
Sumner D. Davis	Birmingham, Alabama
Jack Hirschmann	Minneapolis, Minnesota
Paul Siple	Erie, Pennsylvania
Alden Snell	Washington, D.C.
Clark Spurlock	Eugene, Oregon

During this phase of the competition, the six scouts visited Byrd's expedition ship, the *City of New York*, and met the man who would deliver them to their destination safely, Captain Melville. Honored at parties and luncheons with celebrities and the press, the applicants experienced a whirlwind week. Commander Byrd hosted a final luncheon for the group carefully planned to give him a chance to interact with all the candidates personally. Observing the six with a "Byrd's eye view" would help decide which scout best met the stringent expedition requirements.

All the candidates proved to be exceptional young men. Experienced in winter camping, each scout had earned more than thirty-one merit badges, and several had accomplished great feats. One scout had climbed Mt.

Rainier, one had completed a grueling 180-mile canoe trip, and another had received the prestigious Gold Medal of Honor for risking his own life to save another person.

Paul's achievements, especially his impressive fifty-nine merit badges, almost twice as many as the other candidates, made him a top contender from the start. But it would be Byrd's luncheon that really tipped the scales in his favor.

While some of the other candidates were visibly nervous about being introduced to Commander Byrd, Paul remained poised, confident, and excited at the prospect of meeting his hero. Standing over six feet tall, Paul was a formidable presence, even in his teens. With thick, dark hair framing his face, and a broad, eye-catching smile, he immediately put others at ease. Byrd carefully scrutinized the scouts during the luncheon. Watching Paul, and observing his poise and good-natured personality, made quite an impression on Byrd. Paul's firm handshake also made Byrd take note.

With the six scouts so close in the last stages of competition, the committee asked one final question to determine the winner. The boys were asked "which two they themselves would choose as their companions if it were possible to send three Scouts on the expedition." The other candidates respected Paul, and, recognizing his abilities and numerous accomplishments, every one of them named him as their first preference. Byrd finally had his teen explorer, and Paul couldn't believe his good fortune!

When the committee announced Paul as its choice, headlines appeared in the nation's newspapers, and Paul became an instant celebrity. The excitement in his hometown of Erie, Pennsylvania was evident, and Paul quickly became a VIP. The headline in his hometown newspaper, the *Erie Dispatch-Herald*, illustrated the sense of his town's pride: "ERIE SCOUT WITH BYRD." Family, friends, and even local dignitaries honored him with special parties and events. Following festivities in Erie, Paul headed back to New York for more celebrations with renowned people before beginning his history-making journey to Antarctica.

Two

The Journey Begins

New York City
Summer 1928

Leaving New York Harbor

National interest in the expedition reached an all-time high as the first of the ships, the *City of New York*, prepared to leave New York Harbor on August 25, 1928. *The New York Times* reported: "BYRD SHIP TO SAIL SOUTHWARD TODAY." Paul stood on deck, alongside accomplished scientists and explorers, watching a sea of waving arms and thinking of the journey ahead. Would it be as he imagined? What would daily life really be like at the far-end of the earth? How would he fit in with the rest of the crew? As these thoughts raced in his head, Paul knew only time could answer his questions.

News reporters crowded the docks along with prominent politicians and wealthy businessmen, including representatives of John D. Rockefeller and Edsel Ford, two of the most generous financial backers of the trip. As the crew prepared to set sail by loosening the ship's lines from her moorings, Paul eagerly scanned the crowds. The departure celebration on the docks was chaotic with flags waving, a crescendo of bands playing, airplanes circling in the clear blue skies above, sirens screaming, and whistles blowing simultaneously. This jumble of sights and sounds only added to the rising excitement.

Dizzy from the motion of the throngs of people gathered on the dock, Paul's brown eyes darted quickly across the scene as he searched the crowd for his friends and family. It was a momentous occasion and Paul wanted to be able to share it with those closest to him. He caught a glimpse, turned away and almost as a reflex, settled his gaze on a tiny speck nestled deep within the growing crowd. Narrowing his eyes to focus more clearly, Paul caught a glimpse of the distinct olive uniforms. There they were! Yes! It really was them. Paul's friends from Troop Number 24 were there to see him off on his journey. Paul suddenly felt a deep surge of pride and sense of honor. He had worked so hard to get here, and the scouts—his friends—knew perhaps more than anyone the importance of this moment for Paul. He hoped that his scout mates knew how much it meant to him to have their friendship and support, particularly on this day. The scouts, like Paul, felt a surge of emotions. Knowing Paul as they did, they knew Byrd had selected the right teen for the journey, and they were thrilled to be able to share in Paul's success. Back in his hometown, the *Erie Disptach-Herald* headlines expressed the town's pride: "BOY SCOUTS CHEER AS SIPLE SAILS FOR ANTARCTIC." Despite their enthusiasm, they were still a bit apprehensive about exploring a remote and unknown land. Although they knew it would be a long time until they met again, the scouts vowed to be alongside Paul in spirit for the length of his journey. Their excitement was evident, and Paul was touched by their solid show of support.

Standing next to the scouts, Paul's proud mother, father, and his twenty-five-year-old sister Carrol waved goodbye, their arms reaching out high above their heads, moving back and forth with a singular purpose. Paul's family recognized the inherent dangers of this expedition, but they also knew Paul's resolve would bring him home safely. They were thrilled that he was fulfilling a dream, and despite their anxious nerves, recognized that this was something Paul felt compelled to achieve. It was with a mix of pride and tension that they waved goodbye. With a smile creeping across his face, Paul signaled back with a mock salute, making eye contact with his friends and family one last time before his long journey. Thoughtfully soaking in the moment as the ship prepared to sail, Paul burned the sights and sounds into his memory knowing this would be his last glimpse of home for a long time.

Full Steam Ahead

Finally the *City of New York* lurched forward and steamed her way into the Hudson River. With her wooden hull and coal-burning engine, the gallant sailing ship carried 200 tons of supplies. Under the expert command of Captain Frederick Melville and Chief Officer Charlie McGuinness, the *City of New York* began her long journey south.

It would take a total of four ships to carry most of the explorers and the bulk of the cargo to Antarctica. Amazed by the sheer number of supplies, ships, and men required for the expedition, Paul marveled at the planning required to carry out Byrd's plan. Every ship had been carefully selected for the task at hand, and it was a real feat to coordinate such an endeavor.

Byrd had to orchestrate four ships of different sizes and speeds, all leaving from different ports, and schedule them to arrive at the same location within a single timeframe. Paul knew that organizing a journey of this magnitude required intense analysis and organization. He admired Commander Byrd's ability to bring the expedition from an idea to a reality. Paul knew the expedition team was in good hands and that Byrd had prepared for the journey by anticipating every possible situation that could arise.

In Ship Shape

Byrd had told Paul that the second expedition ship boasted a larger and faster steel hull that could easily overtake the sailing vessel, the *City of New York*. This cargo ship, named the *Eleanor Bolling* in honor of Commander Byrd's mother, made its departure six weeks after Paul's ship sailed. Despite this delay, the *Bolling* would arrive at the rendezvous point in New Zealand first. Under the watchful eye of Captain Gustav Brown, the ship left Norfolk, Virginia, carrying more of the expedition's men and hauling 300 tons of supplies.

Meanwhile, two other ships were also heading to Antarctica, including a steel-hulled Norwegian whaling vessel called the *C. A. Larsen* and another whaler named the *Sir James Clark Ross*. These two ships were assisting in getting the rest of the men and supplies to their Antarctic destination. As all four ships sailed to load their cargoes, Paul thought about the final group of explorers that were traveling by train from New England to Norfolk transporting some of the most precious cargo of the expedition—ninety-five huskies to pull the sledges.

Paul knew that the dogs were eager workers. He had read about their ability to work as a team and use their combined strength to pull the large sledges loaded with supplies sometimes weighing as much as 2,000 pounds. Before this trip, Paul was only familiar with the smaller, more traditional sleds that he and his friends used to play in the snow. The sledges would be a new experience, and one he wouldn't quickly forget.

Byrd selected powerful Greenland huskies, invaluable for hauling supplies and exploring Antarctica's frozen interior, to lead the dog teams. Seventy-nine of the dogs came from Labrador. Arthur Walden, an experienced dog handler who had previously driven huskies in the Arctic Yukon, would lead the group. He personally brought sixteen huskies from his farm in New England. These dogs were well trained to maneuver the large, heavy polar sledges, made of a rigid wooden framework and mounted on runners with the ability to flex over rough terrain.

Byrd personally selected Norman Vaughn, Eddie Goodale, and Freddie Crockett to serve as Walden's assistants. Eager for adventure, "The Three Musketeers" as they came to be known, interrupted their studies at Harvard to join the expedition as dog team handlers and mushers. Just like Paul, the three young men knew this opportunity was very unique and not something that would likely be offered again.

Four days after arriving in Norfolk by train, Walden and his men carefully loaded the dogs onto the *Sir James Clark Ross*. Byrd selected the *Ross* to transport the dogs because of its impressive speed. The dogs were extremely critical to his expedition, so Byrd made every effort to ensure their safety and health. He planned to rapidly ship them through the hot climate zones, so they would not suffer any ill effects from the heat. Paul, a dog lover, appreciated Byrd's efforts to protect the special cargo during the long journey.

Byrd boarded the last ship to depart, the *C.A. Larsen,* docked in San Pedro, California. The ship headed to New Zealand, carrying one hundred tons of supplies, aviation personnel, three airplanes, and fuel for the expedition's aircraft. In New Zealand all four of the ships would meet and restock their supplies. From there, the ship carrying Paul, the *City of New York,* and the faster steel hulled *Eleanor Bolling* would continue on to the Antarctic continent carrying the expedition's men and supplies.

Ships in the Byrd Antarctic Expedition 1928

Names of Ships	Cargo & Men Carried
City of New York	200 tons of material Scientists and explorers Depart New York Harbor Captain Frederick Melville
Eleanor Bolling	300 tons of supplies Scientists and explorers Depart Norfolk, VA Captain Gustav Brown
Sir James Clark Ross (Norwegian Whaler)	95 sledge dogs Dog drivers Depart Norfolk, VA
C.A. Larsen (Norwegian Whaler)	100 tons of supplies Aviation personnel and Byrd 3 airplanes and aviation fuel Depart San Pedro, CA Captain Nilsen

Reflections on the Adventure Ahead

On the first day of the journey, and as the *City of New York* eased across the harbor, Paul felt the weight of his new responsibility firmly resting on his shoulders. Just a few months ago he was a student completing his first year of college back in Meadville, Pennsylvania.

Now, school already seemed like a lifetime ago. Paul realized that in four months he would literally be standing at the other end of the world. He knew he would be up to the task, but that didn't lessen his burden. Isolated at the extreme southern end of the earth in a hostile and unforgiving environment, Paul wasn't merely traveling to another country where just the terrain and customs were foreign. Paul's Antarctic destination would be 2,300 miles from the nearest populated land. There would be no grocery stores, hospitals, gas stations, or familiar landmarks. The only people he would see would be the other members of the expedition team, some of them now sailing on the *City of New York* into the Atlantic along with Paul. All of the little things Paul took for granted in his daily life were suddenly just distant memories.

Paul thought about the adventure ahead and felt both excited and anxious. The Eagle Scout, amid scientists, engineers, mechanics, and dog drivers, was on his way to Antarctica, and it was his honor as an Eagle Scout to be part of this historic journey.

A Commitment to Excellence

Immediately after the *City of New York* cleared the harbor, and as the dock party faded in the distance, Irish sea captain Frederick Melville gathered the men on deck to assign duties. Working from a list, the captain matched each man with a specific job. Paul was assigned to serve as the messmate in the ship's galley.

Heading below deck to his workstation, Paul staggered on unsteady sea legs. As if the swaying ship and the musty salt air weren't challenging enough, he would now have to contend with the smell of greasy food in the warm, poorly ventilated galley situated directly below deck.

With no portholes to peer out onto the horizon, and battling nausea, Paul quickly got to work peeling potatoes for supper. Though he hadn't eaten since early that morning, the constant rocking motion of the ship caused a churning deep in the pit of his stomach. He abruptly sat down, grabbing two pots along the way, one for the potatoes and another in case his breakfast decided to make an unwelcome return.

Despite the blend of strange smells swirling around him, Paul was determined to excel at his first task. Stepping out from the galley and breathing in the fresh salt air after that first meal, Paul's legs were a bit more sturdy, his face no longer pale and drawn. Just as he started becoming accustomed to the smells and motions of the ship, his fate changed abruptly.

After dinner one of the shipmates was shocked to discover a stowaway in the bow of the ship. Everyone rushed on deck to see who had caused the commotion. Standing before them was a young man not much older than Paul.

Chief Officer Charlie McGuinness was charged with deciding the stowaway's fate. Paul wondered why McGuinness paused, looking directly at him. Before the stowaway could spend any time concocting a plausible explanation, the officer quickly turned back to the stowaway, announcing that he would become the ship's new messmate. As was traditional at sea, the stowaway would have to earn his passage and would be put off the ship at the next port—Panama. Captain Melville instructed Paul to escort the new messmate to the galley. Paul would then assume his new position as sailor on port watch under McGuinness' command. Without any fanfare, Paul was just promoted.

During his watch, Paul wondered what new responsibilities lay ahead of him. From the start, he knew the official title of "Personal Orderly to Commander Byrd" was merely symbolic. Otherwise, Paul would be alongside Byrd on the *C.A. Larsen*. Paul wouldn't even see Byrd again until their two vessels met in New Zealand, the final stop before heading to Antarctica.

It was just as well. Paul wanted to earn his reputation as a valuable member of the crew on his own merit. Following along behind Commander Byrd's shadow would have most likely made that more difficult.

After his watch, an exhausted Paul hurried below deck to claim a sleeping bunk for the journey. In the forecastle that housed the ship's anchors, Paul found the bunks. Each one was already piled high with someone else's gear. He looked over at the expedition's carpenter, Chips Gould, and asked where his bunk would be. Chips told him some of the fellows spread their gear over two bunks. He then suggested that Paul clear one off to claim it for himself.

Choosing an upper bunk in the bow with the least baggage on it, Paul moved the pile and jumped onto his newly claimed bed. Not nearly as soft as his bed back in Erie, but it would do for the ocean passage. Before Paul could make himself comfortable, the owner of the gear entered, demanding that Paul surrender the bunk. Paul lay there, unsure of what to do.

When he moved as if to give the man his way, Chips intervened telling Paul to defend his rights. "He has two bunks already. If you want to get along as a sailor, you don't want to be bluffed so easily as that."

At first Paul didn't realize that he was being bluffed. But he did know that it wasn't fair to go without a bunk while another sailor hoarded two. Paul kept his bunk. Though it was a small victory, Paul was glad he stood his ground.

To Paul's surprise, getting comfortable that night took almost as much effort as preparing the first meal. Standing six feet tall and weighing in at 180 pounds, Paul was much too long for the compact five foot triangular bunk that was to be his bed for the next four months. All he learned in scouting didn't include how to fit into such a small space—there was no merit badge for this! He pointed his feet first one direction, then another, even turning them outward. Every position was awkward. Finally, he let his feet hang over the side, but the aisle was so narrow Paul's big feet got in the way. The first few men passing by bumped into his dangling limbs, jarring Paul from his uneasy rest.

His only choice was to prop them up on the bulkhead. There they weren't in the way, but after a while his feet fell asleep. Many nights Paul woke to the prickly sting of a thousand invisible needles tormenting his feet. Paul began a daily ritual of jumping jacks or jogging in place which helped to restore normal circulation in his legs so he was able to walk each morning and fulfill his watch duties. He was beginning to understand why sailors had a reputation for walking funny.

Three

To Antarctica

Caribbean/Panama/Tahiti/New Zealand
Summer/Fall 1928

Disasters at Sea

Paul was initially in awe of his sailing companions, but he would later learn that many members of the expedition team were far less experienced sailors. In order to earn his seamanship badge, Paul had become proficient at rope splicing, navigating with a compass, tying knots, and understanding the complex rigging of a sailing ship. Paul commented later in life that his seamanship badges meant the difference between being "a humble servant and being recognized as a leader."

Paul and the other crewmembers did their best to adjust to the demanding schedule. Day and night the men on watch were required to work alternating four-hour shifts. Being on watch often meant taking a turn at the helm for one hour at a time. This duty proved especially tiring when the seas were rolling as it took a lot of muscle constantly wrestling the wheel to maintain a steady course.

Watch also included lookout duties at night, or daytime tasks such as setting the sails, painting, and swabbing the decks. On the alternating four-hours-off shift the men could eat, sleep, or relax. With this schedule, the men on watch had less than four hours in which to catch some shut-eye. In reality, sleep usually lasted only two or three hours, and most men, including Paul, totaled less than six hours of sleep a day. Despite his growing fatigue, and with his characteristic determination, Paul managed to contribute to nearly every task on board in the weeks at sea before the *City of New York* made her first stop.

The day-to-day routine was soon jeopardized by several disasters. Early in the journey, the wooden hull of the old sailing ship sprung a leak. As rushing water quickly flooded into the engine room, Paul and the other men raced below deck to see what they could do to make repairs. After plugging the leak and stopping the water from pouring in, many exhausting hours followed as they began to drain the engine room of seawater with hand-operated pumps.

The flood set off a chain reaction as other problems began to surface. Salt water damaged the engine and also spoiled part of the ship's precious drinking water. McGuinness reassigned on-board duties so that extra crewmen could work day and night to restore the engine.

With their fresh water now contaminated, the remaining water would have to be rationed. Though crew members always had plenty of water to drink, they were allowed only a half-pail per week to wash clothes. On older sailing ships, fresh water was always in short supply so rationing was not uncommon, but it was still an additional inconvenience.

Bathing and washing clothes in saltwater only added a layer of scum to the existing dirt that accumulated on everything. Before long the men felt grimy and looked filthy. With the salt air clinging to their skin and clothes, their hair became matted like cement. Many of the men cut their hair short letting their beards grow to conserve as much precious fresh water as possible.

A second disaster struck when the radio battery storage room suddenly erupted in flames. Fire on a wooden boat is every sailor's nightmare. A quick thinking Paul, and the ship's radio operator Malcolm Hanson, dowsed the fire before it spread. That night, essentially calm seas barely rocked the ship. Paul rested well, hoping their troubles were over.

Unfortunately, the next morning, the ship was in danger again. The absence of wind had caused her to drift eighty miles off course, slipping across the smooth ocean with the crew nestled comfortably below. Sleeping soundly during the windless night, the *City of New York* began a slow and dangerous drift while a Caribbean storm brewed. Watching as an eerie calm blanketed the horizon, the men received bad weather reports from the coast. Behind them, a major storm was threatening. Florida and Puerto Rico were already ravaged by tornadoes. Destruction on land was extensive, but this time luck was on their side. Thanks to the windless conditions that had thrown her off course, the *City of New York* managed to cut across the ocean safely between storms. Had she stayed on course, the ship would have been in the direct path of the storms and sure disaster.

After three weeks at sea the ship anchored at the entrance to the Panama Canal. Before passing through the Canal the next day, Paul went ashore as the guest of Mr. Elwell, a customs officer and the Scout Commissioner for Cristobal. He took Paul on a tour of the Panamanian cities of Cristobal and Colon. Paul even enjoyed the opportunity to visit the control room of the massive Gatun Locks on the Canal Zone's Atlantic side.

After passing safely through the Canal, Captain Melville had intended to sail the *City of New York* to the next port, Tahiti; however, that evening the engine broke down, forcing her to return to the docks at Balboa on the Pacific side of the Canal for three days to repair the engine. This delay gave a curious Paul an opportunity to observe many of the area's tropical plants and animals, and some locals showed him where to pick wild limes and lemons to flavor the ship's drinking water and to prevent scurvy, a disease caused by a lack of vitamin C.

The next morning in Balboa, Paul was surprised to see that the low dock to which they had tied the ship was now towering above the water. On the Atlantic side of the Canal, tides varied only about three feet, but here the Pacific tides shifted twenty feet or more. Paul took advantage of the delay to learn more about the amazing engineering feat of the Canal's construction and to see more of Balboa and the Pacific side of Panama. Before setting sail once again, Paul toured the ruins of Old Panama, abandoned in 1671 after buccaneer legend Henry Morgan attacked the region.

Bananas and a Rat

The Panama Canal transit brought the crew an unexpected gift from The United Fruit Company—an abundance of green, unripe bananas. In fact, there were so many bananas that a cargo boat had to carry them to the ship. The crew stored them onboard wherever they could

31

find room. They packed bananas into the icebox, stuffed them under the forecastle, and crammed them into every last inch of free space—two hundred bunches of bananas for the unsuspecting men who did not know that in a few days they would all ripen at once!

That week the crew gorged themselves on bananas for breakfast, lunch, dinner, and snacks. Paul and the crew had bananas coming out of their ears. After weeks, the remaining fruit spoiled and was tossed overboard. Even so, the smell was overpowering as it drifted throughout the ship. The rotten bananas also attracted all sorts of tropical insects that had come aboard the ship in Panama. Flies and gnats buzzed around the men's faces, and roaches and water bugs dashed across the walls and deck.

Although the crew hated the bugs, the ship's new mascot thought they were a rare delicacy. Huddled down in the engine room, a crippled, aging rat feasted on a gourmet dinner of water bugs and cockroaches. When too tired to chase insects, the old rat was treated to leftovers from an engineer who adopted it as his pet.

Back in Paul's hometown of Erie, a rat mascot would have seemed odd to say the least, even for Paul who once had a pet crow. However, in this exotic world, even a rat mascot no longer seemed out of place.

The ship had other pets, too. Two stray kittens, named Winnie Winkle and Mary, had stealthily crept on board in New York, quickly becoming symbols of good luck. They both learned early to get along with the rat. Mary eventually left the ship in Tahiti, but Winnie continued to scamper on board, entertaining the crew until she disembarked in New Zealand.

Voyage Across the Pacific

The long trek across the Pacific to Tahiti proceeded uneventfully except for the traditional light-hearted ceremony commemorating crossing the equator, aptly called "Crossing the Line." Playing the role of Davy Jones, Chief Officer McGuinness called upon the mythical spirit of the sea and announced the arrival of King Neptune's Royal Court composed of sailors who had been initiated on earlier voyages. "First-time crossers of the equator" were brought before the Royal Court to be sentenced to a dunking in the water tank and have their heads shaved by the royal barber. Paul hid in a big ventilator pipe watching the fun until he was discovered and sentenced like the rest of the initiates.

As the Royal Court posed for pictures, the initiates caught them by surprise and quickly shoved the members of the Court into the nearby water tank. A water fight ensued but ended quickly when water splashed onto Captain Melville's dress uniform.

Following a forty-day crossing of the Pacific, the *City of New York* anchored in Papeete, Tahiti to take on new supplies. Upon arrival the men exuberantly greeted the crew from the expedition's sister ship, the *Eleanor Bolling*, loading coal at the dock for the next leg of the journey. Although the much faster *Bolling* had left six weeks after the *City of New York,* it easily overtook the slower sailing ship, arriving in Papeete first.

Paul took the opportunity during the short stay on Tahiti to explore the island. "All that has been written about the beauty of the South Sea Islands is no exaggeration," he noted. He particularly enjoyed watching the exotic marine life, and later wrote in his journal about its tropical beauty.

Paul observed "spiny sea urchins, from little greenish purple ones, the size and shape of a chestnut burr, to large black ones, that looked like a crouched-up porcupine. The hundreds of rainbow-colored fish, the size of a pet goldfish, did not seem to mind them in the least."

He spent silent hours in fascination watching "tiny fish more strangely shaped and more beautifully colored than the last. Ruby, lavender, emerald—in short, every imaginable color—inlaid on a background of blue water and brown rocks covered with bright green algae on which the fish were feeding." Having only seen exotic fish in an aquarium display at the zoo, Paul felt lucky to have the chance to observe them in their natural habitat.

Marveling at the dense tropical vegetation and majestic coconut trees during a trip around the volcanic island, Paul re-boarded the *City of New York* as it set sail for New Zealand, the last stop before reaching Antarctica.

En route to Antarctica the ship encountered heavy seas and high winds in the "Roaring Forties," the treacherous waters located between the fortieth and fiftieth degrees of latitude that are famous for rough seas. As the ship pitched and rolled wildly, the call "all hands on deck" summoned everyone to help control her. Paul rushed topside just as a heavy crate of supplies ripped loose, striking him on the head and nearly knocking him unconscious. At that very moment a wave pounded over the side of the ship sweeping him along the deck. Although dazed by the blow he grabbed the ship's rail just before being washed overboard!

"Make the upper topsail fast!" Chief Officer McGuinness ordered. Regaining his senses, Paul scrambled to the top of the mast to help tie down the flapping canvas.

With Paul perched high above the deck, the ship suddenly pitched and rolled toward the threatening water. With the crew watching in disbelief, the mast lurched toward the water while the boat strained against the pressure, dipping the sail into a passing wave. While the men held their breath, the boat quickly righted herself and Paul slowly climbed down to safety. He was relieved to feel the solid deck below his trembling feet.

The work proceeded slowly as the men obeyed the sailors' rule of "one hand for the ship and one for yourself." Eventually the storm slackened and the normal watch routine of four-hours-on and four-hours-off resumed.

Later, on night lookout, Paul thought about his narrow escape from danger. He quickly put it out of his mind as he tried to draw upon the knowledge he'd gained from earning his astronomy merit badge to identify stars and constellations. These observations increased his desire for learning more about the heavens. As a sailor now gaining real-life experience, Paul could use the stars for navigation.

Paul added to his knowledge of navigation and nature by reading books from the ship's extensive library. Books for the expedition crew, donated by individuals and publishers, included volumes of the *Everyman's Library*, *Encyclopedia Britannica*, *Harvard Classics*, several hundred novels, reference works, and a wide variety of books packed with useful information.

On November 26, 1928, the *City of New York* was the last of the four ships to arrive in New Zealand. The ship was a bit battered and bruised from the long ocean passage, so the crew put the *City* into dry dock at Port Chalmers, located ten miles north of Dunedin, for a much needed bottom scraping and hull repairs. Once the ship

Paul Siple at the *City of New York*'s wheel (courtesy Siple Family Collection).

was restored she joined the *Eleanor Bolling* that had arrived much earlier. The two crews spent a frantic week restocking as they loaded the ships with gasoline drums, food crates, airplanes, and even houses.

Earlier that month on November 5th the *C.A. Larsen* had docked at Wellington, New Zealand carrying Byrd and other aviation personnel as well as the airplanes. Crewmembers immediately began unloading the expedition supplies and taking on equipment for its own whale-hunting mission. As soon as the *Larsen*'s crew re-supplied their ship, they planned to head south to hunt for whales outside the ice pack. When the ice pack broke up, the vessel could slip through in search of whales.

Before the expedition began, the *Larsen*'s captain had agreed to tow the *City* through the ice pack only if it didn't delay their hunting expedition and they could rendezvous with the *City* before heading into the icy region in search of whales. The crew of the *Bolling* and the *City* worked furiously loading the expedition supplies so that the *City* could race to meet the *Larsen* to take advantage of this generous offer of a tow through the dangerous and unpredictable ice.

The Norwegian whaler, *Sir James Clark Ross*, carrying the dog drivers and the ninety-five huskies, reached the waters outside Dunedin, New Zealand where it was required to stop and deposit the dogs at Quarantine Island. There the dogs had to remain until the expedition's ships met to continue their journey southward. At that time the dogs were transported by barge directly to the *City of New York* in individual crates where they were stacked along the upper decks of the old ship. This left little room on the vessel for passageways. Excited and uncomfortable, the dogs barked and howled all day and all night throughout the trip south, making sleep difficult for the crew and explorers. The jumble of dogs and cargo added to the rag-tag appearance of the old *City of New York*.

Packed bow to stern with supplies, the *City of New York* and the *Eleanor Bolling* set sail for Antarctica on December 1, 1928. For this leg of the voyage Commander Byrd sailed on board the *City of New York*. A tug towed the *City* out of the narrow channel of Dunedin, and the *Eleanor Bolling* followed astern. Once in open sea the *Eleanor Bolling* passed a tow rope to the *City of New York* and towed her toward the ice pack to attempt a rendezvous with the *Larsen*.

The farther south the ships traveled, the more dangerous the journey became. Icebergs and bad weather were not the only problems, as accurate navigation became more complicated. With the skies growing increasingly overcast, the men were not able to see the sun and stars to establish the ship's position. Because the Magnetic South Pole is located far to the west of the Geographic South Pole, the ship's magnetic compasses become increasingly inaccurate the farther south they sail. The crews could only estimate their location.

Despite the navigation difficulties, the *City of New York* rendezvoused as scheduled with the *C.A. Larsen,* the Norwegian whaling ship that had agreed to tow the *City* through the ice pack toward the waters of the Ross Sea. The plan called for the *Eleanor Bolling* to offload coal to the *City* when they reached the edge of the ice pack and then return to New Zealand for more coal and supplies while the *Larsen* towed the *City* through the ice packs. The tow offered a stroke of good fortune for the expedition. Second in command and chief geologist, Dr. Laurence Gould wrote, "What a boon this tow by the *Larsen* is to us. Without it we should be at a standstill, for with our puny power plant we should never be able to push our way through this ice."

The extended daylight disoriented Paul and the rest of the men. "Everything," Paul observed, "weather and surroundings and time, are all beginning to assume a gray sameness." Transferring heavy bags of coal from the *Eleanor Bolling* to the *City of New York* for eighteen-to twenty-hour shifts interrupted now familiar sleep patterns. To help the men get enough rest and cope with the long days Commander Byrd wisely changed the watch schedule to four-hours-on and eight-hours-off.

Because of its geographic location, Antarctic seasons are opposite from the seasons in the United States and the rest of the Northern hemisphere. When the men reached their destination in December it would be during the Antarctic summer, and the cold not nearly as extreme as it would be in the Antarctic winter that begins in late June.

Seasons in Northern and Southern Hemispheres	
Seasons in United States	Seasons in Antarctica
Spring Begins March 21	Spring Begins September 21
Summer Begins June 21	Summer Begins December 21
Autumn Begins September 21	Autumn Begins March 21
Winter Begins December 21	Winter Begins June 21

Another peculiarity of the Antarctic area is that the sun does not set during December and January. Instead it circles the sky close to the horizon. There is almost no darkness, even at midnight. By one or two in the morning the sun starts rising from its position low on the horizon for another long summer day. Paul and the others soon realized that this almost constant daylight was a difficult adjustment on their minds, bodies, and spirits.

Between long, exhausting work periods, Paul managed to enjoy regular intervals of being on watch, a calmer duty with interesting distractions. During his shifts on deck, Paul spent countless hours gazing at the towering icebergs. Some resembled ghostly shapes while others looked like the ruins of a beautiful city of glass. It became almost a game to imagine the bergs as something other than huge floating chunks of ice. Expedition geologist Larry Gould gave a sense of their magnificence when he said, "I've never seen an unbeautiful iceberg."

During the day Paul also studied the animals that flew and swam near the ship. An avid birding enthusiast, Paul had spent hours in the swamps and woods near his home in Erie and on the wild Presque Isle Peninsula observing birds and taking photographs. Now, looking overhead he watched birds more unusual than any he'd ever seen back home. The most fascinating to Paul were the skuas and petrels. Despite their small size, and unthreatening gull-like appearance, the skuas are scavengers of the air fighting viciously for any food. In contrast, the gentle snow petrels are so white that they blend with the milky sky as they soar overhead. On the ground, they disappear against the backdrop of snow and ice during the breeding season. Paul called these birds the "beautiful ghosts of the Antarctic." Following the ships were albatrosses, soaring the oceans on their huge wingspans of sometimes over ten feet. These great birds spend years wandering the oceans without returning to land except to nest.

The ships crossed the International Date Line at the 180th meridian on the 10th of December, and again on

Christmas Day. The IDL is an imaginary line running from the South Pole to the North Pole through the Pacific. West of the line it is one day later than it is to the east of the line. By crossing the IDL on December 25th, the lucky crew celebrated two Christmas Days.

Four
Arriving in Antarctica

Ross Ice Shelf, Antarctica
December 1928/January 1929

The Ross Ice Shelf

Gathered in the ship's forecastle around an evergreen tree they'd brought from New Zealand and decorated, the men celebrated Christmas of 1928. Although this was an adventure of a lifetime, not being with their families on this holiday made the crew a bit sad as they remembered their loved ones.

The group savored a delicious holiday meal prepared by the cook, George Tennant. Tennant had served as the chief cook on Byrd's North Pole expedition in 1926. Paul enjoyed the dinner, but it sure wasn't his mother's home cooking. Paul really missed her sugar cookies, sprinkled with red and green sugar for the holidays. Physicist Taffy Davies, decked out in a long white beard and bright red parka, livened things up as he played the ship's Santa. Several crew members performed skits, and the group enjoyed singing traditional holiday carols while they opened their gifts.

As the men began winding down their simple cele-bration, the lookout startled them as he called from the

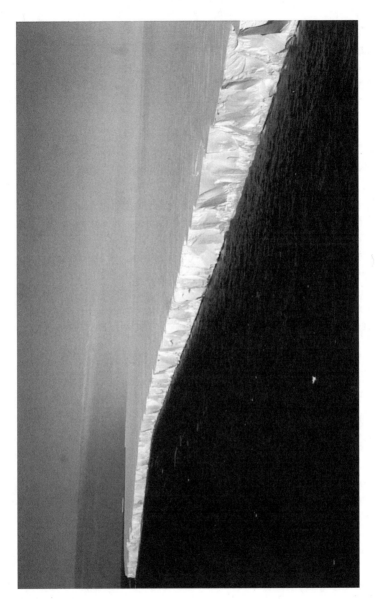

The massive Ross Ice Shelf (courtesy Wendell Wilson Collection).

crow's nest, "Barrier on the starboard bow!" Upon hearing this sudden warning, the crew rushed on deck toward the bow of the ship to receive the best Christmas gift imaginable—their first glimpse of Antarctica!

Admiral Byrd recorded this historic event in his journal. "The thing we had come so far to see was before our eyes, a far-flung reach of lifted ice, stretching east and west as far as the eye could see. In the distance it appeared low and flat, not yet impressive, but there it was—the mysterious Barrier," also called the Ross Ice Shelf. The *City of New York* had crossed the Ross Sea to the Ross Ice Shelf, a mass of ice larger than the entire area of France. As they edged closer to the Barrier Paul saw "a white cliff, rising a hundred feet or more in defiance to keep us from going further south."

The ship turned east along the Barrier and by morning entered Discovery Inlet where the crew hoped to find an area suitable for both anchorage and an airfield. They planned to search further east for Amundsen's abandoned Framheim Base. Norwegian Roald Amundsen, the first man to reach the South Pole, had established his Framheim Base, named after his ship the *Fram*, in 1911 during his overland journey to the South Pole. In addition to its historical and nostalgic appeal, the Base contained abandoned supplies and equipment that Byrd and his men could use for their polar expedition if they could just pinpoint the exact location.

The men watched the Barrier edge calving as great slabs of ice sheared off, falling into the cold sea in a collapse of spray. At the point where an inlet narrowed to two or three miles across, the *City of New York's* crew set two anchors, dropping the metal onto the ice where they grasped tightly into the icy surface. With the anchors now set and holding fast, Commander Byrd headed ashore with a dog team searching for a suitable site for the expedition's base camp.

A Penguin Welcome

When finally able to disembark, the crew wasted no time as they began rushing from the ship that they'd lived on for four months. The freedom of being on a solid surface was exhilarating. They hurried across the ice scooping snow into their gloved hands, running, and tossing it into the air. Even the huskies joined the celebration as they circled the men, barking excitedly over their new freedom.

From a distance the men glimpsed a long ribbon of little black figures approaching. The crew, unsure of what was heading their way, soon realized they were being welcomed by distinguished-looking emperor penguins. Standing at three to four feet high and weighing seventy-to-eighty pounds, emperors are the largest species of penguins. In the bright sun, their square pupils squint to form a tiny diamond shape. The solid black that crowns their head fades to a silvery-gray down their tailcoat. A long purple-edged bill protrudes through the center of a sunset orange face, and its cream-colored feathery chest heaves proudly between long and powerful flippers.

Paul watched as one of the huskies approached the strange birds and sniffed in curiosity. Not interested in making friends with such a strange creature, one of the emperors smacked the unsuspecting husky on the nose. The dog quickly backed away as the penguins waddled closer to the men, then clustered together as if to make an important decision. "We stood silent as they came to

The emperors' welcome (courtesy Byrd Polar Research Center Archival Program, The Ohio State University Libraries, #7766–3).

a halt before us and clustered into a small group," recalled Paul. "With their heads together they appeared to be discussing some important matter. Finally from their long, slender, purple-edged bills came little clucking sounds of approval as they began to nod their heads in affirmative fashion. Then, as with one accord, they turned to face us again."

"One of the largest delegates, between three and four feet tall, and weighing seventy-five or eighty pounds, left the group and approached to within two or three feet of us. He looked at us in a rather approving fashion, nodding his head and clucking spasmodically. Then very slowly he lowered his head upon his breast in a gracious bow, so low that his beak almost touched the snow, and delivered a long welcoming speech that lasted for several seconds and sounded like the clear blare of trumpets playing a range of several notes. Then very, very slowly he raised his head and looked at us with almost amazement in his eyes to think that we had not complied with the request he was trying to convey to us. Believing, perhaps, that he had not stated his request clearly enough, he repeated the performance. Afterwards he looked at us a second time and seeing that we did not comprehend, he began to shake his head in disgust. A critical member of his delegation, who evidently thought this speech had not been properly presented, approached the chairman and nudging him to one side proceeded to deliver the welcoming speech himself, but to no avail. We humans were too ignorant of the penguin dialect to understand what was expected of us. One after another each took his turn with the opinion that he could show the rest how it should be done; but needless to say, they all failed and returned to their little group for another conference. This ended in the agreement that they should leave us dumb human beings to ourselves since we were incapable of understanding such simple statements as had been made to us, and anyway our lack of intelligence would render us harmless. They started to file away in the same solemn manner in which they had come."

The dogs, feeling braver by the minute, tried to corner some of the penguins. Unafraid, a few of the emperors simply slapped the dogs out of the way. Others poked at the dogs with their sharp orange bills.

Paul and the men joined the dogs and tried to catch a penguin. Scared by this attack, the penguins dropped onto their chests and tobogganed away with their strong webbed feet. Unable to run well in their heavy boots, the men watched helplessly as the birds disappeared off into the horizon.

The Ice Cave

While Byrd's group was still out scouting a site for their new home, Paul joined a small band of men on their first land exploration. Four miles across the Bay in the face of the Barrier's cliff they located an ice cave, its entrance framed by a twenty-five-foot arch of hanging icicles. The adventurers roped themselves together, making a long caravan to creep downward into the cavern.

Inside they found a dazzling spectacle as sunlight blanketed the cave's iridescent crystals, setting off an array of blue sparkles. Lace-like ice lined the walls, the slightest touch sending showers of cascading crystals toward the men's feet. Along the cave's floor, glassy spires as thin as strands of hair glimmered. Ice sculptures suspended from the ceiling, some pointing downward like long tentacles, some forming egg-like clusters and still others clinging to the ceiling and walls like intricate spider webs.

Far into the cave the explorers reached a dead end. At the lowest level, they found a seal hole in the ice floor leading to the water below. As Paul and the explorers worked their way back out of the cavern, ice crackled under their boots, the broken pieces forming new patterns on the floor with every step.

Unfortunately, no one had a camera with him to photograph the unusual cave. In the future they would make sure to carry cameras, but they knew they'd probably never find another cave as unique as this.

When the men left the protection of the cavern and began working outside in the freezing winds, they learned how brutal Antarctica could be. One man touched a pipe with his wet hand, his skin immediately turning white, blistering, and freezing onto the metal. Severe pain continued even after he tore his hand away, leaving a large patch of his flesh stuck to the surface.

Others suffered headaches from merely breathing the frigid, dry air. Even those who used caution felt symptoms. Some developed pain in the shoulders and joints caused by a lack of oxygen resulting from a reduced rate of blood circulation. The twenty-five pounds of clothes they wore to ward off the elements pressed against their tender joints inflicting pain at the point of contact.

After exploration of the area, Commander Byrd decided it was an unsuitable site to set up base, as the interior was too hilly for the aircraft to use. After their brief time on solid footing, they cast off their lines, and the ships headed east, entering the Bay of Whales on December 28, 1928.

With careful thought and much consideration, Byrd selected the Bay of Whales as the final destination. Because much of the area was still unexplored, the expedition could claim it for the United States. This site also fit Byrd's larger vision of reaching the South Pole. From this location Byrd's plane would be within flying distance of the Pole. Equally as important, the flat terrain of the Ross Ice Shelf would serve as a reasonably safe runway for Byrd's Ford trimotor. This smooth, low basin also provided a perfect spot for the ship to anchor and for the men to unload their supplies.

Byrd named the inlet Ver-sur-Mer Bay after the French village where he sought help after crash landing his plane during a previous transatlantic flight. The crew docked both ships at the lower end of the inlet, anchoring them with one hundred pound iron hooks that dug deeply into the ice. While Paul and most of the crew remained on board, Byrd and his advance party of six men and two dog teams left the ship to choose a site for their base. The scouting party felt they were near Roald Amundsen's old 1911 Framheim Base but quickly discovered that after seventeen years it had been buried by blizzards. Although they were in the correct location of the abandoned base, the expedition team never managed to uncover it due to the deep layers of snow and ice that kept it hidden well beneath their feet.

What they did find was a protected shallow basin just past the top of the Barrier. On New Year's Day 1929 they returned to the ships with good news. At the higher, inland end of Ver-sur-Mer Inlet, several miles from the unstable ice of the Bay, they found a spot to build their base camp. "Little America," as Byrd named it, would become their home away from home. Paul was eager to begin the next phase of his adventure.

A Whale of a Story

Weather would prove to be just one of the dangers at the Barrier. Curious about tiny black dots moving in the water beyond the Barrier's edge, Paul, Commander Byrd, and a few other explorers took a lifeboat out to investigate. As they headed toward the black specks, someone on the Barrier shouted, "Killer whales!" They would later learn that these "orcas" are the largest of the dolphin family at thirty feet in length. They travel in pods of five to twenty individuals to hunt seals, squid, sharks, fish, other dolphins, and whales. They sometimes raise their heads vertically out of the water, called "spy-hopping," to look about for prey.

Cautiously, Paul and the other three men paddled toward the ice, hoping not to stir the whales' interest. To the men's dismay, three whales swam directly toward the boat. The men turned toward shore. When the whales turned, too, it looked as if they were coming to attack. While Paul and two of the men rowed frantically toward shore, their leader drew his pistol and prepared to shoot if the whales came any nearer. No matter how quickly they rowed, the shore seemed to loom off in the distance.

Finally, after what seemed like an eternity, the boat reached the shore safely. Every man scrambled quickly onto the ice. As a breathless Paul jumped from the boat, a lone killer whale sprang from the water's edge, lunging toward the tip of the ice. Instinctively, Paul leapt backward almost losing his balance. With the whale watching and spy-hopping several feet above the water's surface, Paul gradually inched away from the water's edge and a safe distance away from danger.

By the time the other men saw the whale, it was already fading into the depths and turning to catch the

Beware of "killer whales" (courtesy Wendell Wilson Collection).

other whales swimming away. The pistols carried on the expedition for protection were not needed. Commander Byrd commented that "killer whales aroused dread with their ugly snouts and ominous, triangular fins cutting the water."

A few days before this incident, Byrd appointed Paul to be an assistant to the scientific staff, with the duty of studying animal life. That night at supper the men ribbed Paul about his introduction to this new job, asking him, "Why aren't you out in the Bay studying the killer whales?"

Five
First Tasks, More Troubles

Ross Ice Shelf, Antarctica
Summer 1929

The Barrier Crash

The next morning everyone began unloading supplies from the *Eleanor Bolling*, now moored against a low level shelf of Barrier ice along with the *City of New York*. To haul the cargo from the ship, the crew extended long cables from the *Bolling's* deck to heavy attachments situated on the Barrier. While the men were stacking supplies on the "ice dock," without warning the Barrier began to crack. The weight of the supplies piled on the ice was just too much. With a silent jolt, the ice dock broke into pieces and began floating away.

The men rushed to save the cargo. Jumping from ice floe to ice floe, they hauled the materials back on the ship before they disappeared into the sea. With the convenient ice dock now unavailable to unload supplies the *Eleanor Bolling* had to be moved to the only place left—the towering ice shelf. Crew members reconnected the *Bolling* to ice anchors on top of the icy wall looming far above the ship's deck. They then lashed the *City of New York* to the outward side of the *Bolling*. These towering walls of ice made unloading much more difficult and dangerous.

The work went smoothly for a day and a half when suddenly the crew felt another shock underfoot. A series of tremors followed. Unable to maintain their footing, men slid in all directions, tumbling across the ice as a huge slab of the Barrier broke off and tons of ice crashed onto the deck of the *Eleanor Bolling*. If the ships hadn't been lashed tightly together, the *Bolling* would have easily rolled over from the crushing weight of the ice and disappeared into the watery depths. Instead the ship slowly rolled back upright.

The men on the ice during the crash were thrown hundreds of feet. Benny Roth catapulted over the *Eleanor Bolling*, landing in the icy water. At the same time, meteorologist Henry Harrison, who had been standing farther inland, noticed the icy surface shifting beneath him. With a sudden jolt, the slab of ice on which he stood barreled down toward the water. Thinking fast, Harrison grabbed the anchor chain of the *Eleanor Bolling* as the slab slid past the chain.

Though his quick reaction saved him from drowning, the situation was still perilous. Harrison tightened his grip on the chain, as the ship tilted toward the sea and smashed into the *City of New York*. The *Bolling's* rolling motion tightened his anchor line, leaving him suspended and swaying thirty feet above the water. The other explorers watched helplessly from the Barrier.

In the water, Benny Roth, not knowing how to swim, clung in desperation to a small floe of ice, yelling for help. The ice, too slick to hold onto for long, kept slipping from his frozen arms. Try as they might, the men on the Barrier couldn't see him. The sun's glare was so powerful they couldn't make out any objects on the water.

The *City of New York* and the *Bolling* alongside the Ross Ice Barrier unloading supplies (courtesy Byrd Polar Research Center Archival Program, The Ohio State University Libraries, #7803–2).

Captain Brown of the *Bolling* and Captain Melville on the *City of New York* rushed to lower their lifeboats. The *City's* lifeboat dropped first, but so many men jumped aboard the small craft it almost sank.

With time running out, Byrd and some others risked their own lives by diving into the freezing water to rescue Benny, who was struggling to stay afloat by holding a slippery cake of ice under each arm. It was no use. The water was so cold that the rescuers would surely freeze to death before Benny could be saved, so they were quickly plucked from the water.

Some men hopped back out of the *City of New York's* lifeboat, enabling the remaining rescuers to follow Benny's cries for help. Finally pulling him into the boat, Benny was on the brink of death. His outstretched arms, still dragging the cakes of ice, were like stone. Rescuers rushed the wet victims into a heated room rubbing them down with brandy, the only alcohol they could find, in an attempt to restore some circulation to their frozen limbs.

Meanwhile, Paul and expedition physician Dr. Francis Coman swung a looped rope from the edge of the Barrier, yelling for Harrison to put his body in the rope loop as he dangled by his hands above the water. Harrison finally freed his frozen hands and attached the lifeline. When he released his precarious hold on the anchor line he swung full-force into the Barrier. As Paul and Dr. Coman dragged Harrison up the Barrier wall, the jagged ice further scraped and gouged him.

Although the incident seemed to take hours, it occurred in a mere twenty minutes. Escaping with relatively minor injuries was extremely fortunate for the men, and it was a real miracle that everyone survived the catastrophe. Harrison's hands needed bandaging.

Unloading supplies at the Bay of Whales (courtesy Byrd Polar Research Center Archival Program, The Ohio State University Libraries, #7820–10).

Roth and Byrd suffered frostbite, and tiny yellow patches covered their skin for days.

Everyone's survival enhanced Byrd's reputation as a lucky man. "Byrd luck" was a phrase coined long before this expedition. As far as the men of Little America were concerned, it was helping them now. Early on this journey, Paul had no way of knowing how often he would need that luck himself on this challenging expedition, but as the days wore on, he would soon learn.

Racing Toward an Ice Cliff

Transferring supplies from the ships to the base camp located eight miles inland became the first order of business. Separate duties divided the men into three groups: one unloaded ships, another transported goods on dog sledges, and the third erected the camp. When a minor mishap injured one of the dog drivers, Paul took charge of a dog team. By the time Paul received this change of assignment, the only dogs still available were unruly huskies and rejects, some suffering from the voyage across the tropics. No one believed that these rejects could become productive workers. No one, that is, except Paul!

As someone who had always loved dogs, he set out to learn about his new team and find each one's strength. Pete was a black, white, and brown mongrel. Despite his pitiful appearance, he stood proudly, his fluffy tail curled upward.

Paul's Dog Team

Names	Paul's Descriptions
Holly	"the team leader"
Pete	"backup leader"
Birch	"the worker"
Buss	"the beauty"
Frosty	"the surly one"
Belle	"the pep of the team"
Nuts	"the outcast"
Nova	"once a terrible fighter"
Briggis	"the decrepit one"
Umiak & Kayak	"the Siberian twins"
Lady	"blind in one eye female"
Delilah	"red-headed little vamp"

Holly was a beautiful gray husky. Strong and energetic, she was a natural leader who liked to race along the trails. She could outrun every dog but Birch.

Birch's love of mischief kept him in constant trouble and his dirty yellow coat made him look like an orphan. Buss was the opposite. A husky with a full gray coat and a shaggy tail, Buss was gentle and meek.

That could never be said of Frosty or Belle. Slowed by arthritis and old age, Frosty, a beautiful pure-white husky, was all business. She slept and ate only to rev up for another day of work.

Working or not, Belle was at full energy every waking hour. Though smaller than the rest, she was the most productive. When the workday began, it was Belle who nipped at the other dogs to get them moving.

Paul selected Holly as the first pack leader. He hitched her to the front of the gang-line, a sturdy strap that connected the dogs to the sledge. Then he secured the other dogs in pairs behind her. Because the team followed the example of the lead dog, Paul depended on Holly to remain focused and drive the team forward. Unfortunately, sometimes she got so excited that she ignored Paul's commands. One morning, her enthusiasm almost killed them all.

Holly was excited that day. She raced the team at such a furious pace that Paul couldn't keep her on the trail. As he glanced ahead, Paul experienced a frightening phenomenon common in Antarctica—a whiteout. No matter which way Paul looked—up, down, or sideways—everything looked the same. He had completely lost his sense of orientation! He had heard that when low clouds cover the sky the horizon could disappear. During a whiteout the snow reflects the light into the clouds resulting in the distortion of size and distance. Near objects may appear far away while objects at a distance may seem very close. People and objects in the snow can even appear suspended in the sky.

Disoriented, Paul grew worried as the sledge quickly picked up momentum. They were speeding downhill toward the Barrier cliff. Paul threw all his weight on the brake in hopes of slowing down the runaway sledge.

The combination of Holly's speed, the strength of the other dogs following her lead, and the steep slope rendered the brake useless. All it did was spray snow into the air, creating a flurry that further blurred Paul's vision.

Faster and faster Holly sped the team toward the cliff she could not see. Paul became more concerned. He couldn't stop her! Even if Holly turned sharply when she reached the edge of the Barrier, she would swing Paul and the other dogs over the cliff. Either way, they were racing toward certain death.

Miraculously, Paul wasn't alone. Nearby Dr. Coman, the expedition doctor, noticed when Holly first ignored Paul's commands. Anticipating danger, Coman rushed toward the Barrier's edge to cut off the runaway team. Unable to veer Holly from her fatal course, he threw himself onto the gang-line, eventually stopping the dogs before the Barrier drop-off. It was a close-call for Paul and his dog team. Luckily, Dr. Coman made it through the turmoil in good physical shape. Paul was forever grateful to him for intervening and possibly saving his life. He felt equally grateful for his share of a little "Byrd luck."

Over time Holly learned to reliably take commands. But just as she became a good pack leader, she gave birth, requiring Paul to replace her so she could take care of her puppies. He chose Pete. More determined than any other dog, Pete would thrust his head forward and race, his big ears and shaggy coat swaying in the wind.

As the new pack leader, Pete worked closely with Paul and became his loyal companion. On many mornings, they could be found outside the camp, just the two of them, Paul chatting as Pete sat beside him listening attentively.

Six
Building Little America

Little America, Antarctica
Summer/Fall 1929

Accommodations

It was known from the beginning of the expedition that only forty-two men would winter-over. The others had come along to help unload the ships and to set up camp. Byrd did not make his selection of the men to remain at Little America until a few days before the *Eleanor Bolling* departed for New Zealand to get the remaining supplies. Nearly all the men wanted to stay; however, they understood that everyone except the men chosen to winter-over would leave on the *Bolling*. When Byrd announced his selections for the winter-over group, many men were disappointed but understood that those selected possessed skills above and beyond what the difficult winter would require. Unlike the Antarctic, the northern Arctic bears, foxes, reindeer, seals, walruses, and birds permanently reside with the Eskimos, even during the winter months. But in Antarctica, Byrd's crew and a few colonies of emperor penguins near the area, would be the only winter residents as even the seals, whales, and other sea birds return to the water to escape the harsh winter landscape.

Paul was ecstatic. He had become one of Byrd's elite. He was among those selected to stay. Paul was indeed an "Eagle on Ice!" It was his merit badges that won him a spot in this unique group. His collection of taxidermy and nature badges landed him the job of collecting and preserving seals and penguins for the American Museum of Natural History. In addition to his Antarctic bird and mammal collection he would be the expedition's naturalist, collecting data on the seals and penguins in the Bay of Whales. His own excitement was tempered by sadness, however, when Paul realized he'd be losing so many of his new friends. It was particularly unsettling for the men who had hoped to stay at Little America, the unique remote outpost they helped create.

The *Bolling,* carrying the other explorers, set sail for New Zealand to get the remainder of the supplies in the nick of time. Shortly after the ship disappeared over the horizon, temperatures plummeted, covering the surface of the water in the Bay of Whales with ice so heavy it would have trapped the *Bolling.*

Radio contact kept the forty-two men of Little America updated on the *Bolling*'s progress. Tensions ran high as she fought high winds and waves. She was sailing through rapidly thickening pack ice that remained a constant threat to her fragile steel hull. News of her safe passage through the ice and arrival in New Zealand brought a sense of relief. With a little of the "Byrd luck" the ship and her crew had survived a dangerous trip.

After arriving in New Zealand the men of the *Bolling* loaded three more houses, tractors, and more food onto the ship for her return to Little America. At the end of February, hope for a successful journey back to Little America was dashed. The weather would not cooperate as a thick layer of ice closed around the Ross Barrier preventing the ship from traveling further south. When the *Bolling* turned back for New Zealand the men at Little America knew there would be no more supplies. They would have to make do with what they had on hand. This meant constructing their entire camp out of three houses, three radio towers, and the original supplies from the *Bolling* and the *City*.

For Paul and the others it would be a busy winter. Adjusting to the long winter darkness would not be easy, especially after experiencing a summer where the sun never sets and daylight abounds. The men had to finish building the camp for themselves and the dogs, take their scientific readings, ready the equipment for scientific exploration, and prepare for the flight to the South Pole in the spring when winter storms slackened and daylight returned. They also had to kill seals for their meat. This would help sustain them and the dogs throughout the long winter months. The men felt badly about this because capturing the seals wasn't difficult. They had to put their feelings aside and concentrate on the job at hand—processing and storing tons of meat while the weather was cooperating. In addition to the meat, oil from the seals would be used for heating, a necessity in the frigid Antarctic winter.

Byrd appointed geologist Dr. Larry Gould as second in command of the expedition. Highly respected by everyone on the expedition, Gould took charge of overseeing the construction of the camp, aided by aerial photographer Captain McKinley and carpenter Chips Gould (of no relation to Dr. Larry Gould).

The layout of the camp was simple, yet functional. They built Little America as a triangular-shape by digging three pits four feet below the surface of the snow. Into each corner pit they placed a tall radio mast. The

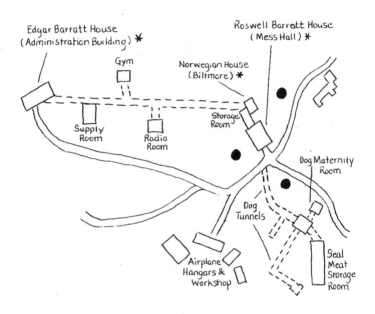

LITTLE AMERICA
ANTARCTICA
1928-1930

Edgar Barratt House
(Administration Building) *

Roswell Barratt House
(Mess Hall) *

Gym

Norwegian House
(Biltmore) *

Supply Room

Radio Room

Storage Room

Dog Maternity Room

Dog Tunnels

Airplane Hangars & Workshop

Seal Meat Storage Room

|| trails

'' underground tunnels

● radio towers

✱ also served as living quarters

towers would relay and receive signals so stations in
America could transmit programs and messages to the
explorers, giving the crew an opportunity to stay in touch
with their friends and families. For electricity the men
placed a wind-generator on one of the camp towers. They

turned off the electricity to the working and living quarters during the sleeping hours while the dog tunnels and storage areas used kerosene lanterns for lighting. However, at minus fifty-five degrees the kerosene in the lanterns often froze, resulting in no light in the tunnels. Even the batteries for flashlights lost power in the cold and had to be kept warm to work. They had a large quantity of coal that would be used for cooking and providing heat to essential areas of camp. More abundant seal blubber and kerosene provided any additional heating and lighting needed. The men also installed telephones to connect the buildings within Little America, marking one of the early uses of telephones in the Antarctic.

The original plan called for five main buildings and a machine shop. Because several buildings were in the hold of the *Bolling*, which was unable to return to Little America with the last of the supplies, everyone would be required to make sacrifices. In the original plans Commander Byrd was to have his own large living area. Due to the lack of housing space for the forty-two men Byrd chose to live in a cramped, ten-foot-wide room that he shared with his pet fox terrier, Igloo (nicknamed Iggy) who had traveled the long distance with his master. The scientists were also supposed to have separate rooms, but lack of building materials meant that everyone lived together except Byrd.

The main structures of the camp were the Roswell Barratt House and the Edgar Barratt House. Edgar Barratt, a New York architect, and his son Roswell had helped plan the buildings and layout but did not go on the expedition. Therefore, for their generosity and support Byrd named the two buildings to commemorate this dedicated New York consulting team.

The Roswell Barratt House served as both an administration building and living quarters for Commander Byrd and most of the scientists. It also contained chief radio operator Malcolm Hanson's research laboratory and Dr. Coman's tiny infirmary. A library with floor to ceiling shelving on three sides was filled with a three-thousand-volume collection of books. Nearby, meteorologists Bill "Cyclone" Haines and Henry Harrison set up their observatories where they would research and gather data on winds and temperatures. Rows of double bunks that slept some of the men took up the remainder of the space.

Sail maker Martin Ronne, serving as the expedition's tailor in charge of creating additional heavy winter clothing and equipment for the explorers, set up his special sewing machine in this area. Byrd had brought along on the expedition a large supply of various animal hides for Ronne to use. His skills were crucial for sewing together the tough hides and other materials that would be needed to help keep the men warm and dry in the extreme winter cold. At age sixty-seven, Ronne was the oldest member of the winter-over party, and according to Byrd, "the greatest craftsman in polar clothing." A seasoned polar explorer himself, Ronne journeyed to Framheim years earlier with Norwegian explorer Roald Amundsen. In 1911, when Amundsen became the first man to reach the South Pole, he used a silk tent built by Ronne. This tent, left behind at the Pole by Amundsen, was found three weeks later by Scott, the second explorer to reach the South Pole.

The Edgar Barratt House served as a large multipurpose mess hall. Long tables and benches filled the main area next to cook George Tennant's compact kitchen. Beyond the tables double bunks for fourteen men took up the remaining space. Always swarming with activity, the building was further cluttered by a tank used for dish washing, shelves lining the walls, a washstand, and a web of clotheslines overhead. In the back of the house was the machine shop, built from airplane shipping crates, where machinist Victor Czegka maintained the airplane parts in preparation for flying after the end of winter.

Another passageway led to the third building, the Norwegian House, where Paul and the rest of the men lived. They nicknamed it "The Biltmore" after the American hotel whose owners donated generously to the expedition, but the room was nothing like the luxury hotel. A large table with upturned boxes for chairs stood in the center of the space. Only one kerosene heater warmed the entire eleven-by-fourteen-foot room. Double bunks lined all four walls. The lower bunks were so cold that the mattress and slats stayed frozen together. Instead of blankets, some bunks were covered with eiderdown sleeping bags. Others, including Paul's, were draped in sleeping bags of reindeer hides brought over from America for added warmth. Clothes were hung on nails driven into the walls. The Biltmore also included a coal bin and a meat storehouse with natural refrigeration of twenty degrees below zero. For Paul, it was a far cry from his comfortable bedroom back in Erie, but it would be home for now.

Toilet areas were built outside the three main buildings. The "refrigerated toilets" were actually deep pits covered by sheepskin seats. These facilities, like the tunnels, were as cold as the temperature outside. To avoid the discomfiting cold, the men learned to wait until they absolutely had to go. Even then, the key to avoid freezing their behinds (literally) was speed. Although the freezing

Little America in the making (note food boxes and radio towers) (courtesy Byrd Polar Research Center Archival Program, The Ohio State University Libraries, #7788–2).

temperature made for a very uncomfortable experience, it at least kept the areas from smelling bad.

Home Sweet Home

The men dug pits and constructed the buildings four-feet below the snow so that the first blizzards would immediately bury the buildings to the rooftops, helping to insulate them from the wind and harsh elements. They dug a tunnel three-feet wide and six-feet deep to connect the two main buildings, the Roswell Barratt Administration Building and the Edgar Barratt Mess Hall. This tunnel became the main artery for the entire camp. Off this central tunnel the men built a twenty by twenty foot gymnasium, as well as separate storerooms for food, meat, medical supplies, coal, and fuel. The tunnels served multiple purposes. They allowed the men to travel within the camp area safely protected from the cold while avoiding the blizzards above them.

Fire was as powerful a threat to the camp as cold weather. If a fire swept through the entire camp in winter the men would be doomed. They constructed the camp so that a fire in one area could be contained and not destroy the adjoining areas of the camp, keeping them as safe as possible.

Vertical shafts leading to the surface snow above stood near the entrance of each building. To exit camp, the men had to climb a wooden ladder, and then lift a trap door opening to the world above.

From the surface, three sixty-foot tall radio towers formed a triangle around the camp. Yet even the three towers were no match for the layers of snow. Once completed, Little America was an under-snow haven with

The Mess Hall, with the Norwegian House in the rear (houses were soon completely covered by snow) (courtesy Byrd Polar Research Center Archival Program, The Ohio State University Libraries, #7803–2).

only the radio masts, black smokestacks, and steaming ventilator pipes breaking the surface.

Completing the base camp called for some ingenuity since many of the supplies and equipment never reached camp. Carpenter Chips Gould designed the machine shop and aviation supply house out of crates that housed the airplanes during the ocean journey. He found parts from another crate to build Malcolm Hanson's radio room. Most impressively, using no nails at all, he constructed a workroom for physicist Taffy Davies out of scraps of wood joined together. No iron could be used in this workroom because of the magnetic studies conducted there.

Throughout the encampment, layers of ice and snow became walls. Within the building and tunnels, seemingly useless materials turned into unique furnishings. Inverted crates became dining chairs, and empty crates became shelves for storage. When the men completed Little America, their ingenious work was the only speck of humanity on the Earth's fifth largest continent—the vast Antarctic.

Seven

Lost

Little America, Antarctica
Fall 1929

The Deadly Blizzard

Most mornings Paul woke to one of two sounds. Usually the dogs' barking roused him. Other times, housemate and dog driver Freddie Crockett blared his favorite song, "Little Coquette" on the phonograph as a wake-up call. Nestled far under the snow in the houses and tunnels of Little America, the men could not see or hear the weather raging above.

Crawling out of his warm sleeping pack, Paul brushed away reindeer hairs sticking to his clothes. He immediately dismissed this common irritation when he learned about the storm outside.

With Little America not yet complete, the men needed barrels of heating oil and other winter supplies that the *City* and the *Bolling* had offloaded at the Barrier. Paul and the other dog drivers were going to brave the gathering storm to bring these critical supplies back to camp before the really intense cold and stormy winter weather arrived.

Some precious cargo had already been covered over in previous blizzards. Almost all the men helped search for these valuable goods, but they were never located. Now everyone felt concerned that more scarce supplies would be buried under the snow and lost forever.

Fifty to sixty mile-an-hour winds swept across the trail connecting Little America and the Barrier as Paul and his friends, Quin Blackburn and surveyor Mike Thorne, stepped outside and hitched their teams. As the three teams started to caravan down the trail, strong gusts buffeted them. The stinging flurries blinded Paul, as he tried to use one gloved hand to shield his face.

As the trek continued, blankets of new falling snow thickened. Gasping for breath Paul struggled to see. As visibility worsened he lost sight of the other two teams and considered turning back. Then, just as he was about to veer his lead dog Pete and the team into a 180-degree turn back to camp, Paul saw an orange trail marker. Paul had designed and built these markers from long bamboo poles with flags on one end. The other end was pushed into the snow to mark trails. On seeing the orange marker Paul was relieved to know that he was only a quarter of a mile from the Barrier. He had come too far to turn back now without the valuable supplies. Paul and his team pressed on, finally reaching the Barrier and re-joining the other two teams who were also having a difficult time.

Huddling together to shield themselves from the wind, Paul, Quin, and Mike loaded the precious fifty-pound barrels of fuel onto their sledges. As the men worked, the storm intensified but they were determined to complete this task. So much snow fell that drifts started to form. If they didn't move quickly, they might lose the trail and be unable to return to the safety of their camp.

Man navigating dog team and sledge over ice (courtesy Byrd Polar Research Center Archival Program, The Ohio State University Libraries, #7782–2).

Lost on the Trail

On the return trip, Mike led, followed by Quin, then Paul. At first they stayed together. As the visibility worsened Paul soon couldn't see them. Using his experience, he watched for the orange flags that had been placed to mark the trail every one hundred yards when visibility was poor. They were his only way to stay on the trail as snow was rapidly burying the trail.

The storm made everything a blur. Paul couldn't see the flags beyond a few feet. After passing one marker, he tried to guide his team in a straight line until the next one appeared.

Now, more than snow blinded Paul. Ice formed around his eyes, making it nearly impossible to squint or blink. He tucked his face into his wind-proof clothing to protect his eyes.

Relying on feel, Paul used his feet to guide him. Whenever Pete veered the team off the trail, the snow underfoot was softer. As soon as Paul felt the change, he steered the team back onto the harder packed snow of the trail.

Soon the sledge began dragging in the thick snow. They were off the trail. Paul turned the dogs and expected to feel the trail under his feet again. The loose packed snow surface never changed, confirming he was lost.

Paul raised his head. He looked forward, to his left, and then to his right. Nothing. He couldn't see the other teams or the trail. He couldn't find an orange flag. The dogs plodded forward. The snow remained thick. In the deadly blizzard, Paul was lost.

The Instinct to Live

Looking behind him, Paul couldn't even see the tracks that the sledge had just made. He wasn't sure which way Pete turned. Despite the sub-zero weather, Paul broke out in a sweat. To survive, he had to make an immediate decision. The wrong choice meant probable death. He had to remain calm and keep his wits about him.

Paul, regaining his composure, suddenly remembered that the dogs hated pulling in a blizzard. To avoid the stinging gusts of snow pelting his face, lead dog Pete would always turn downwind. To get back to the trail,

Paul had to get the team racing directly into the freezing wind. With all his might, he turned the team.

He searched for the trail with his feet. At first, thick snow dragged the sledge. Then he felt a slicker surface under his boots. *This must be the trail*, he thought. He steered Pete onto the icy path.

Watching for a trail marker, Paul guided his team forward. To his relief, an orange flag on a bamboo pole appeared. As the team approached it, Paul realized they might be going the wrong way. If they were heading back to the Barrier, the dogs would not have the strength to get back to camp before the blizzard overcame them.

Paul called again on his scout training, using the wind as his guide. As they pressed forward, he felt the wind whip at his left side. This was how it felt when they were heading toward camp. This must be right.

A few minutes later, a second orange flag assured Paul he was on the trail. He yelled at the dogs to keep going. Then he fell silent. Had he heard something? He wasn't sure. Over the whirling wind and the whining, panting dogs Paul listened. Yes. Well ahead of him Paul thankfully heard distant barking and voices hollering his name.

His dogs heard it, too, for they suddenly turned their stumbling gait into a sprint toward the sound. Within minutes Paul could distinguish the other two teams stopped on the trail waiting for him. They had been as worried as Paul. Now realizing how important it was to stay together, they struggled on until they saw the gasoline storage area off to their left about a half-mile from Little America.

The trail headed straight into the storm. The dogs resisted as it hurt their eyes to face directly into the blowing snow. After a struggle Paul and Mike were able to get their teams to turn into the storage area and drop off their barrels of fuel. Quin's team was a different team than he usually had, and he had a difficult time controlling them. The dogs realized they were close to Little America, and they would not be turned. Instead they bolted and headed for home. Paul and Mike yelled for Quin to stay with them, but Quin couldn't hear them above the howling winds as he fought to control his team. In an instant Quin and his dogs disappeared into the raging storm.

The two teams headed back to camp together. When they didn't see Quin on the trails, they concluded that he must have made it back to camp safely ahead of them. Paul's eyebrows and eyelashes were frozen, and the cold wind caused his head to throb.

Back at Little America Paul had a bracelet of blisters around each wrist where the snow had been driven under his gloves. While Dr. Coman checked Paul over, they learned that Quin was missing.

Like Paul, Quin must have gotten disoriented in the blizzard and turned off the trail. Byrd studied his rescue options before sending out any men. One man was already missing. If he sent out more without taking every precaution, he could lose them, too. As they waited, the men became more concerned. Although the storm seemed to be subsiding, the area would be dark in a few hours and temperatures would drop to a more deadly range.

Byrd made his decision. He and Mike Thorne would go back to the cache, placing flags closer together along their path. Paul asked the commander to let him go, too, but Byrd told him he should warm up from his ordeal before going back into the cold.

After a while, Byrd and Mike returned. They had seen no sign of Quin. Dusk was now only an hour away, and the temperatures were certain to grow colder. Byrd pulled out all stops for a final rescue attempt. He chose four groups of men to scout the area, each following a straight line in a different direction. This time Byrd asked Paul to help rescue his friend Quin. Paul joined the team that was to head downwind toward the Barrier edge. All the groups fanned out to search for Quin. While searching with his team Paul heard distant shouts from another group. Mike skied toward them shouting: "We found him!"

Mike Thorne's group found Quin inside a makeshift trench. After being lost for a while, Quin had realized he could not find his way back to camp alone, so he had stopped his team. With quick thinking and using the resources that were available, Quin used the lid of a box for a shovel, digging a deep hole in the snow and placing the sledge and oil barrels around the trench, blocking the wind. Finally, to avoid freezing he slipped down into the bottom of the hole and gathered his dogs to lie on top of him in an attempt to maintain some warmth. His only hope for himself and his dogs would be to try and ride out the storm buried in the snow.

His return to camp brought relief to everyone, especially Paul. Quin was placed in Dr. Coman's care just as Paul had been a few hours earlier. A staff surgeon at the prestigious Johns Hopkins Hospital in Baltimore and now the official expedition physician, Dr. Coman watched over the boys carefully until their vital signs returned to normal, assuring that neither would suffer long-term damage from their ordeals. Recovering, they shared their stories with one another. Both realized that thanks to their training, strong wills and quick thinking, they managed to survive their frightening experiences. Now the two shared a deep bond that can only come with a narrow escape such as this. "Byrd luck" had held once again.

Eight

Walls of Ice

Little America, Antarctica
Fall 1929

Dog Town

After the mushers hauled all the supplies to camp, they
had a new job, building a shelter to house their dogs for
the winter. Protecting the dogs was an important planning and safety concern. Early in the expedition, the dogs
could stay outside curled in the snow or lying in narrow
trenches, but they would need shelter during the harsh
winter. Soon the sun would disappear, and there would
only be darkness during the bleak winter months. Paul
and musher Jack Bursey took charge of the project.
Bursey proved to be a hardworking handyman, and his
knowledge of construction and repairs complemented
that of Paul's. The two young men always enjoyed working together, so they looked at this task as a challenge.

Besides the huskies that hauled supplies, there were
others that needed special accommodations such as the
newborn pups and the ill or injured dogs. Since arriving
in Antarctica, three of the dogs, including Holly and Belle
from Paul's team, had given birth to new litters.

Working together, Jack and Paul dug a tunnel with wooden shovels toward Ver-sur-Mer Inlet. For two long weeks they scraped through layers of snow and ice, all the while getting to know one another. Jack, having grown up in the frigid climate of Newfoundland, never seemed to mind the freezing temperatures. They dug a ditch about seven-feet deep and several hundred feet in length. Inside the tunnel they carved holes every ten feet and inserted crates so each dog could have a separate sleeping space. With this arrangement, the dogs could move freely on their leashes and enjoy each other's company without being so cramped but not close enough to get into fights.

Along one side of the tunnel Paul dug a separate small room for a maternity ward so Holly, Belle, and Josephine could safely nurse and care for their young. Finally, Paul and Jack covered the tunnels with supporting strips of wood. They then laid chicken wire and covered it with canvas and a layer of snow. Paul was proud of this engineering feat. As a child, he spent many hours watching his dad, an accomplished machinist, tinker in the family garage. Paul was fascinated with his father's ability to fashion a workable tool out of raw metal and now, using his own skill, combined with Jack's talent, "Dog Town" was officially open for business.

Though the tunnel constantly echoed with the yapping of huskies and their newborn puppies, it was a place where Paul spent and enjoyed many hours during the winter feeding and caring for the dogs. Each time he entered, he was greeted with a symphony of barks and yelps, music to his ears. He fed them large chunks of frozen seal meat that required hours of chewing to tear it from the bones. The dogs had very little physical activity in the winter. Eating, particularly gnawing, was their exercise and entertainment.

Once the litters were weaned from their mothers, Paul added table scraps, blubber, and pieces of meat to their diet. Because their thick coats enabled the pups to withstand the cold better than the older dogs, Paul occasionally took them above ground to run and play.

Before long they grew large enough and curious enough to investigate the camp. One night they crept out of their tunnel and followed the scent to the meat storehouse.

Like a scene from a comedy, the dogs were tossing about, knocking over, and ripping apart the entire contents of the room. Most exciting for them, they got their first taste of chicken, turkey, and veal. Before they were caught, they devoured several days' worth of the men's meals.

After that, the young thieves lost their freedom. Paul tethered them to leashes like the other dogs and transformed their old maternity room into a makeshift jail.

Despite the disruption and even the destruction, Paul couldn't stay mad at the dogs for long. Their unique habits and surprising behavior were often Paul's best entertainment. Besides that, he admired their ingenuity.

One morning Paul went in to check on his huskies and discovered something interesting. The dogs preferred to sleep curled up on the ice floor with their bodies melting into the ice as they slept. He realized the irony of his having worked so hard building and inserting the crates so the dogs had their private spaces, only to have them prefer to sleep closer to each other directly on the ice.

The Thawing Room

Following two exhausting weeks of building dog tunnels, Paul was eager to start his winter taxidermy project assigned by Commander Byrd. Byrd explained to Paul that they were expected to return to America with Antarctic wildlife for an exhibit at the American Museum of Natural History in New York City. Paul's contribution would be to carefully prepare the penguins and seals for this important museum display. Although Paul was honored that Byrd chose him to preserve the details of their historic journey, his new assignment was no small task.

Before he could begin his taxidermy, Paul had to gather penguins and find a suitable work area. This project became a bigger challenge than Paul ever imagined. With the help of two Biltmore housemates, aircraft mechanic Pete Demas and his new friend, dog driver Jack Bursey, he dug a seven-foot pit off the main tunnel. He wanted beams to cover the pit, but they were all being used over the dog tunnels. Paul had to get creative. He took a lifeboat left by the *City of New York*, turned it upside down, and had a ready-made roof.

The room needed to be heated enough to thaw the penguin carcasses for dissection and mounting. So while Paul hung large sheets of canvas to create a tent, Pete made a stove that used blubber for fuel out of a gasoline drum. They tested their stove in the completed room. The blubber was so slow to ignite that they spent hours nursing the stubborn fire. Finally it burned steadily and continued long enough for them to go to the mess for dinner. Though leaving a stove unattended was a bit risky, the low flames slowly burning convinced Paul a few minute's absence would cause no harm.

Was he wrong! Gone only fifteen minutes, Paul returned to find flames spitting out of the cramped doorway and a curtain of smoke hovering overhead. Because the buildings were wood, this entire section of the camp was in danger.

With good foresight and a little more "Byrd luck," Paul had moved a fire extinguisher into the tent before Pete Demas had rolled in the barrel stove. Paul leapt into the billowing smoke to extinguish the flames. The sickening fumes erupting from burning rags and seal oil almost knocked Paul unconscious. With the fire still not entirely extinguished, Paul rushed out of the tent, coughing and gasping for clean air.

When his senses returned, he raced back into the tent and pounded out the remaining sparks. Though he put out the fire, Paul's struggle was far from over. The heat from the fire melted one wall of snow, opening a huge gap to the outside. With temperatures of minus fifty degrees the strong winds blew in. Before Paul could plug the hole, the wind rushed in, filling the room with snow.

With Jack's help, Paul shoveled the snow from the tent, but trouble revisited. As Paul began his taxidermy work on the partially thawed penguins, intense heat from the stove again melted the walls, reopening the gap and exposing the room to the harsh elements. The freezing air forced Paul to quit for the day.

That night some of the young dogs caught the scent of the thawing penguins. Sneaking into Paul's workroom and pulling the half-frozen carcasses from the dissection table, they managed to drag them back to their tunnel for a mid-winter feast.

Once more, Paul patched the hole. With the barrel stove breathing heat throughout the room, Paul resumed his work. Because the disasters put him behind schedule, Paul tried to catch up by working until he became bleary-eyed with fatigue. He ran the hot stove all day as he worked day after day. One night, Paul was so tired he didn't notice the heat once again melting a nearby wall, opening yet another new gap.

Exhausted, Paul fell asleep as another blizzard swept through camp. Arriving the next morning to find his workroom packed with snow once again convinced Paul that it was time to find a new workspace.

A Fine Mess

Paul and his partner Jack Bursey began searching the camp for a new workroom. Yet every possible space had walls of ice.

The expedition's cook, George Tennant, was preparing the evening meal as Jack and Paul walked in to ask his advice. Paul shared his story of the recent melting wall disasters.

George kindly offered Paul use of the kitchen when it wasn't being used to prepare meals. The room had solid wood walls instead of ice, and it was warm enough to thaw the penguins so they could be skinned for taxidermy.

Paul felt comfortable in his new work environment, and the hours slipped by without Paul even noticing. Amid the men's grumbles and protests, Paul moved the penguins that were collected for processing to the galley rafters for storage. Within two days, the carcasses thawed and Paul skinned them on George's table.

Next, he salted them to prevent spoilage. Initially it took Paul up to thirty hours to prepare one penguin. With determination, he became so skilled at his job he could skin and clean a carcass in one-third his original time.

Despite his progress, Paul's long work hours seldom lessened. He often worked fifteen hours in a single day, stopping only to let George cook. By mealtime, Paul was usually starving. After hovering for hours over the unappetizing carcasses of his penguins, dinner always brought a welcome break.

Understandably, Paul never felt thrilled when George served penguin, but neither did any of the other men. It had an unpleasant odor and gamey taste that lingered long after dinner. Knowing how Paul hated to eat penguin after preparing their skins all day, George Tennant couldn't help ribbing him by offering to cook him a special dessert—penguin pie! Paul never took him up on it.

Nine
Claustrophobic Winter

Little America, Antarctica
Fall/Winter 1929

Tension in Tight Quarters

The men saw their last glimpse of the sun on the 17th of April. Before it officially set on April 22, 1929, and introduced four sunless months, signs of winter swept across Antarctica. Throughout April, the skies dimmed and the winds blew harder. Temperatures plummeted. Some mornings, Paul and the men woke to minus seventy-degree weather. They always awakened to total darkness.

Gradually the Barrier grew more desolate. First the whales disappeared from the surrounding waters. Within days, the seals were gone too, followed soon after by the orcas. As the third week of June approached, Paul reached the Barrier to encounter a lonely sight. There was a solitary emperor penguin wandering along the ice. Above him, a pair of skuas glided aimlessly across the darkening sky. All wildlife soon left except for some emperor penguins on the ice and Weddell seals in the water. The explorers were the only human life remaining on the entire continent of Antarctica. For Paul, this desolate isolation was an exciting, yet strange feeling.

Passing time during the long Antarctic night, playing cards and games (courtesy Byrd Polar Research Center Archival Program, The Ohio State University Libraries, #7806–5).

Meteorologist Haines kept a chart that showed the freezing, severe temperatures the men were enduring that winter. Temperatures way below freezing were common.

Temperatures Recorded in Little America 1929	
Temperature	**Number of Days**
-72 Below 0	1 (July 28)
-70 Below 0	2
-60 Below 0	33
-50 Below 0	62
-40 Below 0	114

At first, the men overcame the confinement of Little America with strict routines. In the darkness, everyone woke at exactly 8:00 each morning. At 8:30 A.M., they packed into the mess hall in back-to-back shifts for a breakfast of powdered fruit and cereal. As soon as the morning meal ended, everyone worked.

Little America Daily Schedule

8:00 A.M.	Morning Wake-up Call
8:30 A.M.	Breakfast Served in Shifts
10 A.M.-Noon	Work Assignments
Noon-1:00 P.M.	Lunch Served Buffet Style
1:00 P.M.-4:00 P.M.	Work Assignments Resume
4:00 P.M.	Conclusion of Work Day One Hour of Free Time (walking, ski practice, exercise)
5:00 P.M.	Supper with four Seating Times
6:00 P.M.-9:00 P.M.	Antarctic University Lectures Games (poker, blackjack, chess) Reading
9:00 P.M.	Games End
10:00 P.M.	Lights Out Reading in Bunks by Candlelight Writing in Journals
Saturday Afternoon	Radio Broadcasts (KDKA in Pittsburgh or WGY in Schenectady)
Sunday Evening	Movies with Popcorn

In addition to their individual projects, every man shared duties like washing dishes or serving dinner. One of the most strenuous tasks provided essential water for cooking and daily tasks. The men took turns helping fill the snow melter, their only source of drinking water. They made water by shoveling large amounts of snow through an outside hole into a copper tank between the galley stove and wall. The tank held about fifty gallons of snow that would melt down to only fifteen gallons of water. To shave, bathe, or wash clothes, the men melted snow in buckets on their own.

With the water supply so limited, the span between baths increased considerably over time. Some of the men invented a timesaving laundering method they called "dry washing." Instead of actually washing anything, they merely swapped their dirty clothes for other dirty clothes they'd set aside the week before. This style of washing was definitely a new twist on traditional dry cleaning techniques.

The cold temperatures within the bunk areas of Little America made the reindeer sleeping bags essential. Reindeer hair was everywhere and became a real nuisance, as the bags started to shed large amounts of the hair that provided the men with insulating warmth. Often Paul awoke from the irritating reindeer hair caught in his throat. Like many of the men, he coughed up hair that had gotten into his mouth as he slept. Suffering from these frequent "hairballs," he understood what cats must endure. As if the stray hairs weren't enough, Paul and the men had to talk themselves out of the sleeping bags most mornings due to the cold. Once they braved the freezing temperatures, they had to dress quickly, donning layers of thick socks, pants, and shirts before stepping into their mukluks. While they dressed, Paul and the others blew on their hands for warmth before managing to slip their hands into the warm gloves. Paul loved to wiggle his way back deep into his sleeping bag, snuggling against its warmth just a few more precious minutes before emerging to dress in the bitter cold. Undressing each evening was a reversal of this now daily ritual. One can only imagine the difficulty of sleeping and camping on the trail during land expeditions.

By midwinter, the reindeer hair was everywhere. It stuck to clothes, covered the floors, and even had to be picked off the food as the men sat down for meals. Paul and the men would carefully inspect their food for stray reindeer hairs before they ate, spitting out any that were overlooked. Such irritations grew more annoying over the long winter months. For their own peace of mind, the men created diversions to keep them occupied.

The entire camp was far more crowded than originally planned. Many buildings were not delivered when the weather prevented the *Bolling* from completing its final supply trip to Little America. The overcrowding meant there was no privacy. When the weather permitted, the men went out into the snow for solitary walks. These walks were the only way they could be away from the group. Larry Gould later noted that "individual isolation was about the most unattainable thing in Little America."

The most meaningful diversion was starting Antarctic University. More than half the men attended classes two or three times a week. Paul always enjoyed listening to Dr. Larry Gould as he lectured about elementary geology. Paul even looked forward to Gould's frequent quizzes. A professor of geology at the University of Michigan with two summer-polar expeditions under his belt, Gould was one of the most respected and liked men on the expedition team. Paul was no exception as he admired Gould's immense knowledge, easy way and approachable manner, despite his status as second in command.

Harold June tutored on aviation, and the other pilots conducted an aviation ground school. In his radio room beside the mess, Malcolm Hanson explained radio operation and theory. Pilot Bernt Balchen gave boxing lessons in the gymnasium and discussed prizefighters.

Chips Gould discussed maritime law and the merchant marines. Dean Smith talked about snakes. Harrison not only shared his knowledge of weather but also a vast knowledge of baseball and its great players. McKinley focused on aerial surveying.

Paul, missing his studies at Allegheny College with his best friend Alton Lindsey, participated in nearly every class. Paul, along with new friends Jack and Quin, never tired of hearing war stories about the four years Dr. Coman served in the French Army. Dr. Coman knew exactly how to keep the young men's rapt attention and was an expert at recalling his interesting adventures. The young men would hang onto Coman's every word, begging for more until it was time to turn in for the evening.

Antarctic University Course Overview
Little America
1928–1929

Aerial Surveying	"Cap" McKinley
Aviation Ground School	Harold June
Baseball	Henry Harrison
Boxing	Bernt Balchen
Geology	Dr. Larry Gould
Maritime Law	Chips Gould
Radio Operation	Malcolm Hanson
Snakes	Dean Smith
War Stories	Dr. Francis Coman
Weather	Henry Harrison

Paul especially enjoyed his sparring matches with Balchen in the gymnasium. To increase his agility and power, he joined several other men in daily workouts that included weightlifting and calisthenics. Always athletic, Paul played football and ran track in high school. He liked to work up a sweat and felt energized by the physical activity.

Exercise routines were often interrupted by friendly contests. At age forty-one, Byrd set a camp record for the most one-handed chin-ups. As soon as someone broke his record, he began challenging the others to wrestling matches. One evening, the hulking Norwegian sledge-maker Sverre Strom accepted. He flung Byrd over his

Enjoying the warmth of the Mess Hall (courtesy Byrd Polar Research Center Archival Program, The Ohio State University Libraries, #7806–6).

shoulder, tossing him into an iron stove that cut a huge, bloody gash into Byrd's forehead. Needless to say, this incident toned down the wrestling matches.

Minor events like daily meals became celebrations. Despite the men's frequent reminiscing, and imagining the flavors and aromas of their favorite foods enjoyed back home, George Tennant's cooking was a treat no man took for granted. He baked fresh bread each week, and his entrees consisted of everything from whale, fish, seal, or penguin, to the barreled beef donated by the skipper of the *C.A. Larsen*. Favorite side dishes included macaroni, prunes, and bread and butter. It was a little taste of home that the men savored each day.

The men particularly appreciated George's cooking skills, especially when compared to what they ate otherwise. When they were hauling supplies by dog teams, they ate Eskimo biscuits, tasteless three-inch squares of pressed vegetables and fat that were hard as concrete. Not much better was pemmican, a frozen block of compressed meats and tallow. Although loaded with protein for energy, the greasy pemmican tasted strong and unpleasant. It was so rich that if eaten by itself it could cause nausea, so the men improvised, shaving it into thin slices and mixing with hot water to make a thick soup, then eating it with a roll. Pemmican doesn't spoil and has vitamins added to it to prevent scurvy that can result from a diet that lacks vitamin C. It was during these bland meals that Paul longed for one of his mother's home cooked suppers. Just the thought of her Sunday steak, cooked rare just as he preferred, accompanied by a salad topped with radishes straight out of the family garden, an ear of fresh corn dripping with butter, homemade yeast rolls, and a tall cool glass of iced tea complete with a sprig of mint could set his mouth watering.

Little America Menu

Breakfast
Eggs
Ham
Oatmeal
Canned Fruit
Prunes
Bread and Butter
Molasses, Syrup
Coffee, Tea, Cocoa

Lunch
Assorted Cheese
Sardine or Salmon Sandwiches
Coffee, Tea, Cocoa

Supper
Soup
Side Dishes
    Macaroni, Dehydrated/Canned Vegetables such as
    Potatoes, Onions, Spinach, Beets, Carrots
Main Course
    Mutton, Roast Beef, Pork Roast, Chicken, Penguin,
    Seal, Whale
Dessert
    Pies of Mince, Apple, Pumpkin, Custard
Coffee, Tea, Cocoa

Every Sunday George prepared a special dinner, such as a huge pork roast followed by a snack of popcorn and orangeade served during the "Sunday Night Feature." In reality, their great cinematic productions were a few old movies on a reel-to-reel projector. Eventually the men watched the movies so often they knew every frame and line of dialogue by heart. In time, the men's side comments became more entertaining than the movies themselves.

The only regular event that surpassed the Sunday movie was the Saturday afternoon radio broadcast. Each week, Malcolm Hanson's radio picked up an hour of music and entertainment from KDKA in Pittsburgh or WGY in Schenectady. Though the reception was poor and seldom lasted throughout the entire broadcast, the men gathered to listen and wait for the pauses between comedy routines and musical numbers. It was then that the station relayed messages from family, girlfriends, and friends to the men at the bottom of the world. Paul looked forward to messages from his mother and father back home in Erie.

Despite the miles, the men were also able to get regular news reports from home, thanks to *The New York Times*. The paper transmitted nightly press releases to Little America that were then copied and posted on the camp's bulletin board. Reading the postings each day helped the men feel at least somewhat connected to their homeland. The bulletin board was always thriving with activity during the evening hours as the men read, pondered, and discussed the news events. During previous expeditions, men had to wait until the ship returned for them at the conclusion of their expedition to receive any news from home, and by the time it was received, the news was outdated by months and even years.

When they weren't listening to news, the men played records on the phonograph in the library. Favorite songs like "Chloe," "The Bells of St. Mary," and Al Jolson's "My Melancholy Baby" were played over and over again. The small collection also contained jazz and classical music.

Besides listening to music some of the men took refuge in the library to read. Housed in the administration building, the library featured an iron stove, comfortable chairs, good lighting, and thousands of books. The donated collection, selected by Dr. Gould, offered the men a wide array of subjects to read about and to help pass the time. Predictably, Gould chose many books about earlier polar expeditions and literature about Antarctic explorers including Shackleton, Scott, Amundsen, and Nansen, as well as science and philosophy. The men frequently used the *Encyclopedia Britannica* for reference, browsing, and to settle arguments.

They gravitated toward fiction as much as nonfiction. A few of the men even enjoyed reading poetry while others loved the classics from the *Everyman's Library*, including works by Charles Dickens, Rudyard Kipling, and Mark Twain. The men also enjoyed more contemporary fiction. They favored stories with tropical settings, especially their favorite, *Green Mansions*. Published in 1904, the novel by W.H. Hudson is a tragic love story set in an exotic South American jungle. They also liked westerns by Zane Grey, murder mysteries, and detective stories. Paul read all the polar books and for a change of pace, selected works by James Thurber, his favorite humorist.

One person who used the library daily was mechanic Pete Demas. By volunteering for the job as night watchman, he could divide his time between watchman duties and reading. Each half hour during the long night, he would also observe the aurora, a bright glow in the sky, and check and record the velocity of the wind. As a precaution against fire, twice each night he made the rounds to check the houses, trails, and tunnels. The rest of the time, Demas could enjoy the quiet of the library, sip his thermos of hot coffee, and read his favorite O. Henry short stories. As one of the most studious explorers, the airplane mechanic also devoured scientific books, technical manuals, and even tackled classical philosophy if he didn't feel too tired on the long nights alone.

Many evenings Paul would sit with Martin Ronne, the expedition's sail maker and tailor and oldest of the explorers. Byrd selected Ronne for the expedition because of his expertise in designing, repairing, and making polar clothing. Paul watched in wonderment as he crafted clothing to keep the crew warm and dry. Much of the clothing was made from reindeer hides Byrd had brought along on the expedition. Ronne had spent time with the Eskimos and observed how they used their natural resources for protection from the freezing temperatures.

Ronne brought these ideas to life with his needle, thread, and special sewing machine, using the skins to craft everything from parkas and sleeping bags, to footwear and pants. Although the men brought cold weather clothing with them, Ronne's polar clothing ensured the safety of the crew and allowed them to work outside for long periods of time, protected from dangerous frostbite. Mukluks, the winter foot gear, were made of reindeer with canvas over-boots.

In the summer when the weather was more tolerable, they wore mukluks fashioned out of sealskin. Boots were made a bit larger than regular shoes to accommodate felt inserts under the foot and three to four pairs of socks for added warmth. Pants were made of windproof canvas-like material or reindeer skin. The same material was also worn over the reindeer and fur parkas. The parkas themselves consisted of reindeer hides with large hoods trimmed in fur. The oversized hoods protruded out over the men's faces, shielding them from the bitter wind. Fur mittens protected their hands from frostbite and were designed to easily remove, making the fingers easily accessible for tasks where a grasp or fine motor skills were needed. A variety of facemasks made of leather, wool, or other materials were tried as a way to protect noses, the delicate skin around eyes, lips, and even eyelashes. Without this type of protection, even Paul's eyelashes would freeze quickly and tightly in the bone-chilling cold.

Paul was amazed at the simple, yet effective clothing Ronne made. As a scout, he always looked forward to winter camping but never dreamed he would be doing it in Antarctica, wearing reindeer fur no less! Later in life and inspired by Ronne's skills, Paul would go on to direct research of Arctic clothing for the military.

Except for the night watchman, all the men retired to their bunks at 10:00 each evening. No records played, no radio screeched and crackled. In silence, the men read, wrote letters, or updated their journals by the light of kerosene lamps or candles. It was in this solitude that Paul could reflect upon his day in his journal and write notes regarding his specific assignments during the expedition. With no Sunday comics to enjoy, Paul also used this time to draw his own cartoons.

These quiet moments offered small relief during the tense winter. Nonstop togetherness forced the men to look for ways to get along. Despite the absence of privacy, the men found consolation in having so many colleagues at camp. When one man grew tired of being around some of the others, he could always find another group to work with.

Commander Richard Byrd inspired the men to be loyal to him and to each other. Previous polar expeditions were usually more similar to the military, where rank

Paul in his Antarctic clothing, including full-length parka (courtesy Siple Family Collection).

created a barrier between the officers and the non-officers. But in the close living conditions of Little America Commander Byrd used a democratic approach marked by a relaxed and more casual relationship between the leaders and other men.

Having nowhere else to go beyond the camp was as much a solution as a problem. Being with each other twenty-four hours a day for many months made the men determined to avoid confrontations and resolve conflicts. Even Paul felt the tension of life in such close quarters. At home he could slip into his upstairs bedroom, adorned with his favorite bird and animal photos, taxidermy work, and hand-painted merit badges that lined the top of the walls, to read, write, or draw. Here, there were no such luxuries.

One day Paul was in the gymnasium when he witnessed a simple disagreement between two men flare into a near fistfight. Rigid with fury, the men stared nose-to-nose, their fingers curled into fists. Paul, who got along with everyone and had a calm demeanor, was about to rush toward them to stop the fight when one man's shoulders relaxed. The other man stepped back and released his anger with a sigh. "Forgive and forget?" one said, extending his hand. After brief consideration, the other man shook hands. "Forgiven, forgotten." Then they returned to their workout. Paul was relieved that the pair resolved their conflict without his help.

Companions

Despite his easy-going manner, Paul tired of the long winter. Back home in Erie, winter camping had been one of his favorite pastimes. His trips had been relatively short and mostly limited to an occasional three-day weekend. During those brief trips Paul filled every minute with activities such as setting up camp, hiking, studying plant and animal life, cooking, and reading before breaking camp and returning home again. Here in Little America the days passed slowly as one day blended into the next, the weeks becoming months with no end in sight. Hours of work and library reading became boring and tedious.

Paul, along with Quin and Jack, spent some of the free time improving their skiing skills in preparation for the spring exploration. Sometimes, when the weather allowed it, Paul looked forward to taking long solitary walks in the snow around the camp. This was the time he used to reminisce about his friends and family back home in Erie.

Some of the men enjoyed playing bridge and hearts, but by far the most popular evening pastime was poker. Without money, the men wagered their cigarettes or chocolate. As one of the few men on the expedition who didn't smoke, Paul was never issued any cigarettes. He loved chocolate so much that he ate his allotment long before poker night arrived. As a result, he never played poker.

One night it seemed just as well. In mid-game men's tempers ignited. As a petty squabble started, Paul left the tense mess hall to take refuge in the tunnel with his dogs. From his first weeks in Little America, Paul enjoyed the companionship of his sledge dogs.

Throughout the lonely winter, Paul appreciated their loyal companionship. In the depths of their tunnel, the dogs came to life when Paul arrived to feed them. Their response lightened Paul's heart and made him grateful for the close bond he developed with his canine companions.

Ten

New Dogs

Little America, Antarctica
Spring 1929

A Sad Parting

One of the primary goals of the expedition was for geologist Larry Gould to lead a geological survey team 400 miles south into the interior of the continent where the Queen Maud Mountains rose majestically above the ice and snow. Rock samples would answer many questions about the age and geology of the Antarctic continent.

Dog teams were critical to this exploration. The expedition's use of a snowmobile, equipped with caterpillar treads, proved to be unreliable compared to dogs, and the men ended up abandoning it far from camp after its final breakdown. Traveling such a great distance required large dog teams to haul the men and supplies. Paul's team was one of the five needed, so he turned over his dogs to surveyor Jack O'Brien for the Gould party trip into the southern interior.

Losing his team of beloved dogs disheartened Paul. However, knowing that Jack would be their new master consoled Paul, at least a little. Paul liked him personally,

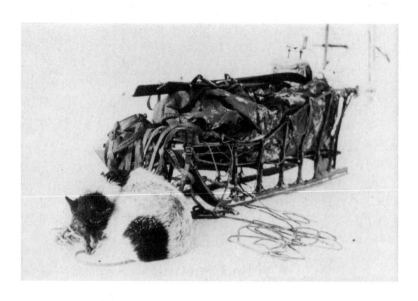

Sled dog takes much-deserved break (courtesy Byrd Polar Research Center Archival Program, The Ohio State University Libraries, #7788–4).

and Jack could be trusted to provide well for the team. Paul had observed Jack's natural ability with the dogs and saw how they responded to him favorably. For his part, Jack respected Paul and knew that the dogs were not only well trained, but that they spent many hours in Paul's company, playing and serving as loyal companions. Jack wanted the dogs to feel as comfortable with him as they did with Paul, and he would do his best as their new master to earn their trust and loyalty just as Paul had.

On the night before they departed, Paul brought the dogs out of their tunnel and gave them the seal meat that they loved so much. He spent as much time as he could that evening with his dogs—Jack's dogs. He played with

Belle and her pups, racing them up and down the trails branching out from camp. He petted Holly until her own pups demanded her attention. And finally he sat back and had one of his long, familiar conversations with Pete. It was a bittersweet parting as Paul felt both pride and sorrow. Although he was proud that the dogs were selected for this important assignment, he was also deeply saddened that they were leaving the camp and he wouldn't have his canine companions to care for and rely on for companionship.

The Princess and the Peons

Paul needed another dog team to train. Though nowhere near the quality of his best dogs, there were a few shaggy or rejected dogs left at camp by the Gould party surveyors. To Paul's surprise, amid the unhappy outcasts were two dogs from one of his previous teams: Briggis and Delilah.

Briggis was never hard to find. Besides being the most pitiful looking dog Paul had ever seen, he was also the noisiest. As soon as Paul entered the tunnel to make his selection, Briggis started yapping. Though energetic, he was also weaker than most of the huskies at camp. He had very little hair and shivered constantly in the cold. Briggis was so thin that for a long time Paul thought other dogs were taking his food from him. Later Paul realized that Briggis was probably infested with parasites, an untreatable condition in their circumstance.

Unlike Briggis, Delilah was a beautiful dog with red hair and deep, dark eyes. The surveyors rejected her because she was vain and uncooperative. Among the dogs

"Cool" husky (courtesy National Archives, College Park, Maryland).

left behind, however, she was the one with the most potential. Paul selected her as the new pack leader and placed Briggis right behind her during their run.

The rest of the dogs didn't offer much variety. Most of the dogs that worked throughout the last season were now gone with the surveyors, as were the larger male pups born to Holly and Belle. But still remaining were Josephine's seven little females, all just a few months old. The seven sisters completed his new team.

Seven Sisters

Of the seven, only the three all-yellow dogs, Canopus, Chi, and Bluey, looked anything alike. Australis was the only sister with perked ears. Sirius, with her brown coat and pure white face, most resembled their mother, but Stella was a red dog similar to Delilah. Yet the most beautiful sister was Dinny whose white nose and collar punctuated a jet black body that glistened in the sun.

When it came to training these dogs, Paul knew the odds were stacked against him. Besides having the most unruly dogs imaginable, Paul had no training in the art of dog breaking. What he did have was patience and determination.

Paul's New Dog Team
"The Seven Sisters"

Australis	Dinny
Bluey	Sirius
Canopus	Stella
Chi	

Leaders: Delilah and Briggis

Dog master Arthur Walden told Paul that training these dogs was a hopeless task because young pups would not be able to do more than four miles a day until they were older, and there was no good leader for the team. Byrd jokingly told Paul that he might want to use Iggy, his tiny pet fox terrier, as a lead dog. Paul appreciated the humorous suggestion. After all, Iggy was the size of an average housecat and forever making an escape from his master, ending up in Dog Town with the fierce huskies. Iggy definitely possessed the attitude of a lead dog but proved no match once a scrap ensued. After these encounters, stubborn Iggy would lick his wounds and limp back "home" where Byrd and Dr. Coman patiently waited to patch him up again until his next adventure.

Paul listened politely to the advice but ignored it as soon as he returned to the dogs. What choice did he have? He needed a team that badly.

To Paul's relief, Delilah responded with enthusiasm to his pep talks. Her large paws shifted eagerly after Paul hitched her to the sledge. She waited anxiously as Paul harnessed the playful pups as well. With Briggis right behind her barking, Delilah set off on their early trial runs with vigor.

The pups did the unexpected. Instead of fighting the restraints or dragging along behind Delilah and Briggis without pulling, they helped pull the sledge from their first run. Soon the misfits became a respectable team. Briggis found confidence as Delilah's backup. With her new responsibilities, Delilah became a good leader. While never very maternal to the younger dogs, she acted more like a patient teacher. She encouraged their progress and tolerated their mischief.

For a while Paul also showed great patience concerning their antics. When they yapped and played when they should have been working, Paul tried to rationalize that they were still just puppies. But over time, their misbehavior grew destructive. Their worst habit was chewing themselves free from their harnesses. Sometimes they shredded them so badly it took Paul an entire afternoon to mend the tattered straps. From past experience, Paul knew that such shenanigans could not only be disruptive but could also endanger them all.

Eleven
Seals

Ross Ice Shelf, Antarctica
Spring 1929/Summer 1930

Weddells and Crabeaters

With spring's improving weather most of the work shifted outdoors. Knowing that Paul was interested in wildlife, Byrd asked him to study and record the growth and behavior of baby seals being born on the ice at the Bay of Whales. Byrd had assigned Paul's friend Quin Blackburn the task of surveying and mapping that same Bay, so the two young men agreed to join forces. Paul's new dog team would haul their equipment to their new jobs. They had worked together many times before and always enjoyed each other's company. Besides that, they both had near fatal experiences during the fall blizzard, and although they rarely spoke about it, that experience drew them closer together as fellow explorers. They were becoming seasoned veterans of Antarctica.

Paul helped Quin with his survey work by erecting guide markers made of blocks of snow piled head-high at prominent points around the Bay of Whales. In return, Quin helped Paul record the measurements of the growth of baby seals. Together they hauled the necessary scientific equipment by dog team to the study's various sites. During these trips they often discussed sports, reminisced about their friends back home, and speculated about what their families were eating and doing at this very moment.

They particularly enjoyed studying the Weddell and crabeater seals. Weddell seals are chubby, reaching eleven-feet long and weighing as much as 1,200 pounds. By cutting breathing holes in the ice under the large frozen fields extending from land, they are able to stay farther south in the winter. Weddells exist on a diet of fish, squid, and krill and are able to catch Antarctic cod that weigh over 150 pounds. With small faces and very large eyes they can see in the deep, dark winter depths under the ice. The females are good guardians of their young and very protective.

The crabeater seals also thrive in the frozen waters, and there are more of them than any other type of seals in the Antarctic. When first discovered it was thought they ate crabs, but one of their main food sources is actually krill, a shrimp-like crustacean. Smaller and more slender than the Weddells, they grow to nine feet in length and 500 pounds. Their fur is cream colored, and sometimes they are called white seals.

Paul found the seals as fascinating as the penguins. One October day while working at the Bay of Whales, a large pregnant Weddell seal surprised Paul and Quin when she emerged from her exit hole, waddling across the ice toward the survey markers they were building. In the minus twenty-degree weather, the seal gave birth to her pup, which was covered with brown wool instead of short black hair like the adults.

Paul's first order of business was tagging the baby seal's flippers for identification. Once done, Quin held the baby seal while Paul measured its length, a task he repeated at regular intervals to chart the seal's growth. In addition to the total length, he also measured the pup's head, body, and flippers.

For these measurements, neither the baby seal nor its mother objected at first. Paul and Quin weighed each pup by putting it into a net fastened to a scale and the pup didn't resist. But the mother seal eventually became enraged at seeing her baby restrained and acted very protective.

Paul and Quin were so focused on their first weighing that they never saw their attacker approach. The female Weddells seemed to have a natural skill of attacking when it is least expected. Afraid for her baby, the mother seal lunged her 1,200-pound frame forward. With her mouth opened wide, she snapped her jaws within inches of Paul's back. The loud clap she made with her teeth caused Paul to jump, almost losing his balance and sliding below the net where the seal pup remained suspended.

Calling upon his agility as a football player, Paul managed to roll out of the way just in the nick of time as the pup slipped free of the net, dropping onto the snow below. Even more furious now that her baby fell, the mother seal began thrashing left and right, snapping loudly at Quin and biting at Paul.

Paul leapt to his feet, bumping into Quin. Together they ran backward as the mother continued to snarl and bark, gnashing her teeth between snaps at their legs. The protective mother seal didn't calm down until her baby seal nuzzled safely beside her.

Convincing the mother that they were not a threat proved impossible. Stubborn and persistent, the mother seal remained focused on keeping her baby away from the strange intruders she did not trust. Paul and Quin gave up on the first weighing session, but later found a tactic that worked. Paul or Quin, or their third helper, the much admired and respected Dr. Coman, would distract the mother seal while the other two quickly attained the weight and measurements of her baby.

Paul was never so grateful to see newborns as he was the morning some other seals gave birth. This time, he tried unsuccessfully to find a mother who was neither as hotheaded nor stubborn as the first. However, it became a three-person job requiring one man to distract the mother seal as the other two weighed and measured the baby seals.

Paul tracked the growth and development of ten newborns. Though only fifty pounds at birth, they grew rapidly. After only two weeks, the infant seals each weighed more than one hundred pounds, and the thick wool that covered their bodies shed, leaving only the short hair of adult Weddells.

Around this time, the mother seals lead their young to the exit holes, or to open leads of water, nudging them in for a swimming lesson. They guide their attentive pups through some basic maneuvers, using their flippers to propel them and jutting their head upward and then side-to-side in order to gauge their progress in the water. Then the mother seals paddle to protected waters and watch their young practice, with ever growing skill, what they just learned.

By the fourth week, the young seals master every aspect of swimming except getting out of the water. Over and over the mother seals demonstrate the maneuver, made difficult only because it requires strength that the pups, now more than 200 pounds each, have not yet fully developed.

Paul observed that the mother seals dive down into the depths of the Bay when they see their baby pups struggling to get out of the water. This allows the mothers to get a racing start. Then swimming up under their pups, the mothers literally toss each pup's heavy, chubby body up onto the ice.

The seals' rapid growth astonished Paul. By the end of his first month of observations, they were bigger than he. Their teeth also surprised Paul. When they cut them at about three weeks old, the seals can immediately use their teeth as powerful cutting tools. Unlike other skills which they learn from their mothers, the seals instinctively know the strength of their teeth and employ them to gnaw holes in the ice for entry and exit holes.

This natural skill made Paul's job more difficult. Paul could grab the newborns, touch them, even bundle them in his arms to get them into the scale net. Once their teeth came in though, Paul had to be careful just reaching for them. Less out of fear than playfulness, the seals snapped at Paul's hands while he was working with them one on one, or at his heels while he worked with another seal.

Some baby seals loved the attention and responded to the measuring and weighing as a game. While this made the seals a joy to work with, it also proved a nuisance when Paul and Quin were done measuring.

These young seals refused to be dismissed. When Paul and Quin began working with another seal, they would squirm toward them, nudging the other seal aside. When that failed, it demanded their attention by barking.

Seal on ice floe (courtesy Wendell Wilson Collection).

When a little petting failed to satisfy, it started nibbling at Paul and Quin's heels.

For a while, they could continue working with the minor irritation of teeth scraping at their boots. Finally one pup perched up on its flippers and, with its mouth open wide, raised itself unsteadily and lunged at Paul's buttocks. From then on, Paul never turned his back on a mother or baby seal.

While the young seals became more aggressive, their mothers grew more accepting of their human intruders. Instead of attacking, they were content to remain a good distance from Paul and Quin and voice their objections with a symphony of odd sounds. Their clicking teeth sounded like castanets. Sometimes they croaked like huge bullfrogs. Other days they chirped like canaries. Most often, they bellowed, sounding like a cross between a mooing cow and a baaing sheep. Paul and Quin enjoyed a friendly competition of guessing what sound the mother seal would make next but eventually lost count of the score.

Paul also studied the crabeaters and their newborn pups. The crabeater is unique in the animal kingdom. Because it eats almost nothing but crustaceans, its teeth are shaped "like a white oak leaf with a number of lobes with cuts between that run almost to the center of the tooth. The side teeth are triangular-shaped, and instead of hitting as our molars do, they intermesh to form a sieve when the jaws are closed so that a mouth full of crustaceans can easily be strained out of the water."

Although this teeth structure is ideal for their diet, it does little to help them defend against predators. Because the crustaceans they eat are inch-long shrimp-like creatures called euphausia, a common krill species that lives in the cold ocean surrounding Antarctica, the crabeater seals must hunt for food in the very realm where predators are present.

As a result, the tame-looking seals are actually very tough. When Paul was close to the crabeaters he noticed the deep scars covering their bodies, earmarks of earlier narrow escapes from predators.

Unable to attack the predators, the crabeater seals instead release their aggression by attacking other seals, particularly the Weddells. Once, Paul and Quin witnessed just such an attack, and Paul recorded in his journal: "The agile crabeater tore at his clumsy opponent with his long front teeth. The Weddell seal could not move fast enough to defend himself and kept rolling over on his side, away from his aggressive foe. Finally he headed for his hole, hitching his corpulent body along as fast as he could. The crabeater chased him to the hole snapping at his flippers as he went." Because the crabeater's teeth were small, the Weddell escaped with only minor wounds.

After seeing the defenseless Weddell struggle, Paul took extra pains to handle them gently. In time, he and Quin even spoke to the seals the same way they talked to their teams of dogs. Though not expressive and responsive like Pete, Holly, or some of the others in his team, the seals nonetheless grew more cooperative, and working with the seals went more smoothly.

While away from camp on these assignments, Paul and Quin managed to get in a few moments of fun too. If there was time before they had to return to camp, and they weren't too tired, they formed "footballs" out of densely packed snow and took turns playing quarterback and wide receiver, keeping score of their touchdowns. As a former high school football player, Paul enjoyed this break from their work routine. This "football stadium" was like no other on the face of the earth.

Twelve
Attempting the Impossible

Bay of Whales, Antarctica
Spring 1929

A Partnership

Paul felt as happy as Quin to have help with his team and new job. On their runs, Quin sprinted with Delilah, tugging at her harness whenever she veered from the trail. Delilah seemed less distracted by the unfamiliarity of the route than by the unruly pups. While they loved the freedom of racing to the Bay of Whales day after day, they never quite grasped that they were working. To them, harnessed or not, they were at play.

Once they started, neither Paul nor Quin could stop their mischief. To the young men's frustration, it took only one pup to create a tangled mess. Even with Paul pushing the brake and Quin slowing to a trot, the dogs pressed forward until the leather ropes became so twisted that the pups literally dragged to a halt.

Paul and Quin didn't think untangling the dogs could make matters worse. They were wrong. While both men worked to free the pups, one-by-one they gnawed through their restraints and took off running in all directions. As

119

one man untangled the dogs, the other gathered the runaways.

One morning Byrd asked Paul to take him on a run to the South Barrier with the other teams to see how the new group was faring. The thought of Byrd riding behind his unruly team caused the pit of Paul's stomach to knot. His misfit team had problems in every trial run. Paul's only hope came from switching to an experienced lead dog. Byrd said he could use Holly for this run.

Although it was less than eight miles it would be his team's first long trip. Paul gave the other teams a half-mile head start so his young dogs would not interfere with the other team by trying to play with them. With Byrd along for the first time, Paul and his team headed to the Barrier.

The Wildest Ride

To Paul's relief, the trip with Byrd began quickly but uneventfully as the pups broke into a running start. The puppies took well to Holly, and her focus kept them working together. They even sped past some more experienced teams. Eventually, however, one pup became distracted, and the chaos began. While careening to one side to play with the sister beside her, the mischief-maker tripped on the gang-line, became entangled and was dragged along.

She yelped as if being tortured. Paul yanked on the brake. It was useless. The dogs were running too fast. As the rest of the dogs ran forward, the hapless pup, still screaming for help, got more tangled in the lines. Seeing Paul struggle, Byrd helped him pull on the brake. A half-mile later, their combined effort stopped the team.

Paul dove straight toward the terror-stricken pup, battered from having been dragged along the ice. The resilient pup, more frightened than hurt, got back to work immediately. As Paul untangled and realigned his pack, the more experienced teams sped past them. With their competitive juices still pumping, Holly and the puppies bolted. Their take-off yanked the sledge and overturned it, catapulting Byrd high into the air. He landed several feet behind Paul. Unaware of their destruction, Holly and the pups kept running in an attempt to catch the other dog teams.

As the capsized sledge scraped past him, Paul managed to grab hold. Dragging across the ice, Paul strained to turn the sledge upright. With all his might, he tucked his legs and sprang upward, ramming his shoulder into the sledge. It righted with a thud. Startled, the runaway team came to a screeching halt.

Paul crept toward his dogs so he wouldn't stir them into yet another frenzy. Within minutes, Commander Byrd, shaken but uninjured, caught up with the stalled team carrying an armful of shovels and crowbars that were tossed with him from the sledge.

Paul and Byrd anchored the team by driving the tools into the ice and tying the gang-line to them. Then Paul untangled the dogs.

He quit thinking his dogs could make a good impression on Byrd. By now he just hoped that their wild antics wouldn't kill the Commander. When Paul and Byrd loosened the crowbars and shovels and got back to the sledge, the dogs did it again.

As if a starting gun went off in their heads, all the dogs took off. The sledge jumped over the crowbars holding it in the snow, and together, Paul and Byrd jammed down the brake. It was no use. The sledge was speeding much too fast. They let go of the brake and flew onward to the Southern Barrier, Byrd stunned, Paul defeated, and the dogs thrilled to be racing in the wind. When the team finally tired, Paul was able to regain control. Byrd called it the "wildest ride I ever had."

Paul left Byrd with the others at the Barrier and returned to his team for the trip back to camp. While he had been with the men the dogs had occupied themselves by chewing apart the sledge's lines. Nearly every dog was now loose again.

After capturing the dogs, it took Paul a full hour to knot and mend the straps. He eased the team across the ice. While the dogs proceeded at a steady pace, Paul thought his hasty patch job would hold until they reached Little America. Then the gang-line snapped. Paul scooped the dragging line with his gloved hand and then dropped onto the ice, hoping his weight would stop the team. Though hungry and tired, the dogs still rushed forward.

Blood seeped through Paul's gloves as he pulled himself hand-over-hand to the back row of dogs. Since his weight alone couldn't stop them, he thought maybe dragging him and the back dogs would tire out the rest. Even this didn't work.

Once again, Dr. Coman came to the rescue. Seeing Paul's struggle, Coman, risking danger himself, drove his sledge diagonally toward the spot Holly was approaching. Just as he had managed to stop Paul's former team, Coman dove onto this one.

With his hands dripping blood and now nearly frozen blue, Paul struggled alone to mend the harness. As much as the doctor wanted to help, he had to stand on the sledge brake to keep the dogs in place until Paul completed his repairs. Paul found himself once again thanking Dr. Coman for saving his life. It seems that Dr.

Coman was always in the right place at just the right time!

Despite the calamities witnessed by Commander Byrd and suffered in private, Paul felt proud at the end of the day. Against all odds, he had taken a pack of misfit puppies and completed his first run to and from the Barrier, a task the other men insisted couldn't be done. Unruly, undisciplined, and unfocused, the seven little sisters did the impossible—they covered fifteen to twenty miles in one day.

Thirteen
Byrd's Historic Flight

Little America and the South Pole
November 28–29, 1929

Preparing to Fly

Beyond exploring regions and recording scientific data about weather, topography, and animal life, the main historical purpose of the expedition was to be the first to reach the South Pole by air and to photograph the unexplored terrain. For months, as Paul worked with the other men on the preparations for the surface exploration of the Bay of Whales region, Commander Byrd and the aviation team prepared for what would be their record-setting flight.

Fate, as it had so often, lent a hand for Byrd's landmark flight. At noon on November 28, 1929, Dr. Gould's geological party exploring south of Little America along the proposed route of flight radioed a weather report: "Unchanged. Perfect visibility. No clouds anywhere."

Meteorologist Haines reported to Byrd saying in effect, "If you don't go now, you may never have another chance as good as this." As if inviting Byrd, the sky opened, and the wind calmed.

Years of planning had gone into preparing for this moment. Completely focused on the job ahead, Byrd ordered the Ford trimotor fueled and made ready for the flight.

Byrd went to his quarters and emerged with an American flag weighted by a stone Byrd had found near Floyd Bennett's grave. His friend Floyd Bennett had been on his first historic North Pole flight. Symbolically, he would be on this one, too. Upon reaching the South Pole the flag was to be dropped from the plane to mark the historical achievement.

The Bull's-eye of Disaster

Several men were loading the plane as Byrd arrived on the airstrip. At the last moment Byrd decided to add another one hundred gallons of gasoline, bringing the weight of the *Floyd Bennett* up to the maximum amount it could take off with.

This decision caused some concern among the men. They all knew about "the hump," and wondered if that extra gasoline would make the *Floyd Bennett* too heavy to climb above it. Two glaciers, the Liv and the Axel Heiberg, led to "the hump," a sharp incline at the lip of the polar plateau. Both glaciers were in the path to the South Pole. Extra weight would lessen the performance and range of the airplane, limiting its highest altitude needed to clear the glaciers. Every effort had been made to reduce the plane's weight.

But Byrd believed that the extra fuel could give them the added flying time they would need should they encounter unfavorable winds. After all, the ideal conditions, with light headwinds at twenty miles an hour and clear

Digging the *Floyd Bennett* out of the snow hangar prior to the historic Byrd flight (courtesy Byrd Polar Research Center Archival Program, The Ohio State University Libraries, #7763–18).

skies currently being reported by meteorologist Haines, may not last. There was no way of knowing what the actual weather was like along their route between the glaciers and the South Pole.

Following hearty goodbyes, navigator Richard Evelyn Byrd and aerial photographer Ashley McKinley entered the plane where pilot Bernt Balchen and pilot/radio operator Harold June were waiting. With excitement racing through their blood, the four men took off for the South Pole in the *Floyd Bennett*. At 3:29 P.M. on November 28, 1929, after a thirty-second takeoff run on skis, the *Floyd Bennett* lifted slowly into the air. The first part of the flight would be above the trail of the Gould survey party that was traveling by dog sledges to examine the lands to the south of Little America.

Throughout the flight to the Pole, Paul, Quin, and the other men delayed their work assignments at Little America to huddle around the radio listening for the progress of the *Floyd Bennett*. The men on board the plane radioed at regular intervals during the trip. They were dependent on their sun compass for navigation since magnetic compasses were of little use due to being so close to the South Magnetic Pole. The sun compass would use the sun to guide the trimotor to the South Pole. They passed Mile 20 Depot and then Mile 44 Depot, two significant landmarks that the Gould party had used to store supplies. This confirmed that Byrd's sun compass was performing perfectly.

By flying the trimotor ten degrees left of their course to compensate for the winds, the *Floyd Bennett* was on the planned route to the South Pole. All three engines were running smoothly. If even only one engine were to fail, the *Bennett* would be too heavy to fly and would have to make an emergency landing. Back at camp, the men remained glued to their radios in silence, holding their breath in anticipation.

Cruising to the south of Little America, the crew of the *Floyd Bennett* sighted the Gould party, and the trimotor descended to 750 feet. Over Gould's men the fliers released a parachute containing a package of treats, radio messages from home, and letters from Little America—the first Antarctic airmail. On an earlier preparation flight Byrd observed that "some of the men were in harness, pulling with the dogs and the sight of their bending backs, the operation of the sledges, the very, very slow progress told everything. If ever a conclusive contrast was struck between the new and the old methods of polar travel it was then."

Soon the flight was over crevasse country. In that region, layers of snow-covered holes and wide cracks in the ice sometimes hundreds of feet deep. Land parties couldn't detect them until someone literally crashed through the bridges of snow hiding the crevasses. Such falls could send men and dogs plummeting to their death. The *Bennett* was able to safely fly over these dangerous traps.

After passing the Gould party the plane began a full throttle climb to maximum altitude. Byrd positioned himself behind pilot Balchen to decide which glacier they should fly over.

Byrd had to choose between two options: the Axel Heiberg Glacier, which Norwegian Amundsen had climbed in 1911 and whose highest elevation had already been established at 10,500 feet, or the unexplored Liv Glacier, whose elevation had not been determined. The heavily loaded *Bennett's* maximum height was going to be very close to this altitude. Scientists thought Liv might be lower, but no one really knew the height of this unvisited land.

Byrd's decision now was pivotal. The wrong choice could lead to catastrophe. With no prior records to draw from, Byrd had to base his decision on logic and instinct. Once again, fate stepped in to help provide the answer.

Balchen pointed out a thick fog that rose over the ice of Axel Heiberg. As his eyes took in the ominous sight, Byrd distinguished further trouble. He noted cloud layers in the same direction, so Byrd decided to attempt flying over the unknown Liv Glacier that was in the clear. They turned toward Liv Glacier, now looming wider and, they hoped, lower than the Axel Heiberg.

Heading aft, June refilled the tank with the last of the extra fuel Byrd had requested. As pungent fumes filled the cabin and burned their eyes, June tossed the empty cans overboard one by one. Each empty can sent overboard meant only one pound less weight, but each pound was precious to clear the glacier. June subtracted the extra pounds that dropped out of the plane with each released can.

June finished his calculations and confirmed that the headwinds had caused them to consume extra fuel. Byrd had been right. The extra gasoline added at the last minute meant they now had enough fuel to reach the Pole and return if they made it over the mountains.

As the *Floyd Bennett* continued its final climb to clear the glacier's edge, turbulence rocked the plane and nearly sent McKinley tumbling out the photography hatch. He grabbed the edge of the hatch, squirmed backward, and closed it tight.

As Balchen veered left and the plane steadied, the men fell silent. They detected an anxiety in Byrd's voice that wasn't there before. Then they knew why. Huge mountains bursting through the glacial streams hemmed in the Ford trimotor. The only route to the Pole was through the pass and straight ahead.

Loaded as she was now, the *Floyd Bennett* flew below the altitude it needed to clear the glacier. Suddenly they were soaring straight toward the bull's-eye of disaster.

Balchen pulled back on the controls, and the Ford buffeted as it tried to rise higher in the sky. The nose dipped as the airspeed decreased. He pulled back again, but the heavily loaded trimotor could climb no higher.

Up and down, tossed and rattled by the strong turbulence from the winds swirling around the mountains on either side, the small plane was trapped between two mountains, heading for an outcropping that it could not rise above. They charged unavoidably toward it, unable to turn around in the narrow pass.

"X" Marks the Spot

Byrd considered his alternatives. Pilot/radio operator Harold June jumped toward the emergency release valve of the main gas tank. If they dumped the 600 gallons of gasoline, the plane would rise above the immediate danger but would not have enough fuel to reach the Pole. He turned to Byrd.

Balchen was yelling something. Due to the loud engines echoing off the mountain cliffs, communication was by shouting or written notes. Though all the men strained to understand him, the roaring engines now running at full power drowned out his garbled cries. He gestured frantically, but his movements were as unintelligible as his shouts. Yet, Byrd understood the message. Of course, something had to go overboard. Byrd yelled to June, "Harold, a bag of food overboard!"

June signaled to McKinley. "Shall I do it, Commander?" he shouted. Byrd nodded. With one powerful lunge of his foot, McKinley jettisoned a huge 125-pound bag of food overboard. The plane responded instantly, rising several hundred feet in the air.

Even with that relief, Balchen knew it was not enough. They were still below the outcropping and heading straight for it. Byrd ordered another box of their survival food overboard.

McKinley raised his eyebrows questioningly, and Balchen repeated, "More!" McKinley responded just in time. As soon as he dropped the bag, the plane rose again. The massive glacier that had stood before the men was now a little below them. With Mount Nansen's black precipice at the left and the steep cliffs of Mount Fisher on the right, the *Floyd Bennett* scaled over the gap between them so closely that McKinley saw the bag burst on the glacier and its contents scatter on impact.

The men were now totally committed to the flight as they were too far away from Little America for any rescue attempt and did not have enough food to live on if forced to walk back. There were no seals, penguins, or other sources of food in the desolate Antarctic plateau beneath the aircraft. Death by starvation would be inevitable. They watched the frozen terrain pass by. With engines now humming steadily, the *Bennett* skimmed along 1,500 to 2,000 feet above a level polar plateau with no higher terrain visible toward the South Pole that was only 300 miles ahead.

Though earlier explorers had climbed past the peaks and onto the polar plateau, the men in the *Bennett* were the first in history to see this land from above. McKinley resumed taking photographs to document and share this historic event with the scientists and the world.

The chain of mountains across the left horizon, with their craggy black rocks streaked with snow, were the most impressive of sights now that they posed no danger. Later the pictures could be used to calculate the height of the mountains they flew past. For more than a year, solid white had consumed every image across their Antarctic landscape. The contrast of dark and white was breathtaking.

The artful and unique sastrugi, the parallel striations in the snow caused by wind, were equally impressive. From their aerial vantage point, McKinley found them a perfect photographic subject, and Byrd studied their direction and depth, ideal indicators of wind speed and changes in the airplanes drift that would be helpful in maintaining course.

The *Floyd Bennett* was now flying level at 100 miles per hour above the high Polar Plateau that surrounded the South Pole. As the mountain range disappeared behind them, the air cleared. Based on the airplane's position in relation to the sun, Byrd calculated that the South Pole was only fifty-five miles straight ahead.

Shortly after midnight on the early morning of November 29th Byrd announced that they were directly over the South Pole. His radio message sent from the South Pole to Little America said: "My calculations indicate we have reached the vicinity of the South Pole. Flying high for a survey. Byrd." To ensure that they didn't miss their mark, Byrd and his pilots flew the plane in a straight line for several miles in four directions, making a huge imaginary "X" in the sky over the point they determined to be the Pole. Covering the sky for so many miles in all directions guaranteed that, even if they were off slightly on their calculations, they would unquestionably fly over the South Pole.

In the center of the "X" Byrd released the American flag. Weighted by the stone from Floyd Bennett's grave, Old Glory floated to the ground just as Harold June radioed Little America to share their success. The men shouted in jubilation. Of all their achievements on this expedition, this was the greatest. Paul and his colleagues were as excited as if they had flown themselves. Just being part of the expedition team for this historic flight was reason enough to celebrate.

The *Bennett* then reversed course. Wishing to fly over new, unexplored lands, Byrd suggested they return on a path a little to the east of their southbound route and directly toward the Axel Heiberg Glacier. Clouds appeared off to the right, and it would be a race to reach the glacier before the clouds. With a large amount of fuel used up, the *Bennett* was lighter and faster now. By climbing to 12,000 feet they were able to pick up a tailwind of twenty-five miles per hour. They won the race with the clouds and glided down over the Axel Heiberg Glacier to a landing at the base of the glacier where a fuel supply had been stored. They refueled and a little over one hour later took off for Little America. At 10:00 on the morning of November 29th the radio towers of the camp were in view, and just eight minutes later the *Floyd Bennett's* skis touched down from her world record flight. The men had been gone eighteen hours and thirty-nine minutes. A jubilant celebration followed.

On this eventful day, little did Paul realize that in years to come there would be an American station at the South Pole, and he would be its first scientific leader. Relieved and thrilled to see his hero return, Paul asked Commander Byrd: "What was the Pole like?"

"A white desolation and solitude," Byrd replied. Paul closed his eyes, trying to envision a seemingly endless

Commander Byrd in the library prior to South Pole flight (Byrd dropped the stone, wrapped in the small American flag, from his plane while over the South Pole to honor his friend, Floyd Bennett) (courtesy Byrd Polar Research Center Archival Program, The Ohio State University Libraries, #7778–1).

and colorless plot of land barren of life. Forgetting about the celebration going on around him, Paul kept his eyes pinched tightly, hearing only silence while allowing his mind to transport him to the Pole. He felt at peace.

Fourteen
Setbacks and Celebrations

Ross Ice Shelf, Antarctica
Spring 1929/Summer 1930

Penguins Found—and Lost

Following the successful South Pole flight, Commander Byrd told Paul that he hoped to bring live penguins back to the United States and give them to zoos across the country. During the winter Paul had completed the taxidermy task of preparing several species of penguins for a prominent place in history: they would be among the star attractions at the American Museum of Natural History in New York City.

For this final phase of his naturalist assignment, Paul needed to collect two species of penguins, emperors and Adélies, for transport back to the United States. The emperors were the larger at three to four feet; the smaller Adélies were about two-feet tall. Both species can waddle upright or for faster travel lie on their breasts and use their feet to push themselves forward. They are both terrified of killer whales and leopard seals that prey on them in the water. On land they are fearless, because they have never known any danger above water until man and sledge dog. The Adélies are particularly confident and challenge even the sledge dogs, usually losing the contest.

With a caravan of dog teams and help from his colleagues, Paul formed a penguin-catching party. Gathering the emperors would be easy, as they were large and rather slow on land. The Adélies, however, would be difficult. Swift and spunky, Adélies were alert and determined birds.

One afternoon not long after their arrival in Antarctica, Paul was helping to prepare the single-engine Fairchild airplane known as the *Stars and Stripes* for a test flight when he saw an example of how determined an Adélie could be. As the engine revved, the men noticed a tiny black dot racing toward the plane. It was an Adélie. The little penguin rushed right up to the giant metal bird and studied it curiously. It stared at the long ski feet and looked up at the buzzing motor.

Afraid that the penguin would get hurt, the men tried to chase it away. Adélies will not be chased. Instead, they will stay and fight, no matter how big their opponent. Finally, one man caught the little visitor, ran him to the edge of the Barrier, and flung him as far into the water as he could.

The Adélie was not about to be tossed away. Like a torpedo, he soared out of the water and shot back onto shore. Before the man could grab the stubborn Adélie, the penguin rushed back to the plane. Unfortunately, the penguin got right into the slip-stream of the propeller as the pilot revved up the engine for takeoff. Squawking wildly, the Adélie was spun around and around, then was thrown several yards, landing in a heap on the ice.

Now it was really enraged. The bird stalked back to the plane ready to fight. By the time the Adélie returned,

Adélie penguins (courtesy Wendell Wilson Collection).

the plane was already speeding away. The little penguin rushed to attack the big metal bird, but a flurry of snow scattered by the plane pushed him backward again. With his unfriendly new opponent lifting off the ground, the Adélie gave up. Turning, dropping to his breast, and pushing with both feet he scooted back to his water home.

Thanks only to the number of men that Paul had helping him, he was able to capture fourteen emperors and six Adélies for his penguin study. Back at camp, Paul devised a plan to keep them contained. He dug two deep pits separated by a gate.

All the penguins remained in one pit until feeding time. Then one-by-one Paul released a penguin from the crowded pit, hand-fed it, and then let it roam in the second pit. To Paul's dismay, the penguins were so unhappy with their new diet that they refused to eat. He tried

Emperor penguins (courtesy Wendell Wilson Collection).

giving the penguins hot dogs, sardines, and several types of canned meat. They wanted none of it. Finally he cut long strips of seal meat and blubber that the penguins seemed to tolerate. Unfortunately, because penguins eat their food under water, it does not occur to them to catch and pick food up from the ground. As a result, Paul had to hand-feed them, sometimes literally pushing food down their throats so they could swallow.

Poor appetites did not diminish the penguins' energy. They immediately started working on their escape. Whenever Paul left them alone, the penguins chipped sections of the pit wall with their sharp bills. In no time they formed crude steps that led them up and out of the pit.

After their first escape, Paul corralled more penguins, and then surrounded the pit with a picket fence

More emperor penguins (courtesy Wendell Wilson Collection).

made of split bamboo. The new barrier couldn't stop them. After pecking a new set of steps, the penguins pulled out the pickets with their bills. The second group of captives found freedom, too. Later Paul would realize that in nature this "pecking of steps" was the same skill penguins used to climb upward onto floating ice high above the water.

Paul tried to ensure that the third group would not outsmart him. This time he lined oil barrels around the pits. Too close to squeeze between and too heavy to push over, the barrels would surely keep the penguins secured.

But the penguins remained one strategy ahead of Paul. Frequently Paul stopped by the pit to make sure the penguins were still there. At first, they looked about innocently. *Too innocent*, thought Paul. Later that evening, Paul crept silently toward the pits. When he peered

More Adélie penguins (courtesy Wendell Wilson Collection).

in, he saw one penguin keeping watch while the others poked furiously at the ice to build new steps. As soon as the penguin on lookout saw Paul, he squawked, signaling the others to stop their work. When Paul stood above the pit, they moved about casually as if nothing was happening.

Later that day, Paul again sneaked to the pit and was shocked to see penguins popping out of the pit and gliding back to their Barrier home. Paul rushed to figure out how they were able to spring so high. The tallest penguin was standing on the highest step. The other penguins were getting a running start and racing up the steps, onto the penguin's back, then up and over the barrels. They were working as a team. Paul suddenly recalled his high school track team. The penguins reminded him of his fellow hurdlers!

Paul hurried to round up the latest escape artists. It was no use. As soon as he would catch one, several others had freed themselves. After a frantic effort, Paul gave up. If they fought that hard to regain their freedom, then Paul believed it was well deserved.

Before trying to gather another group, Paul decided instead to tell Commander Byrd about the penguins' astounding escapes. Maybe they didn't need to be brought to the United States after all. In the end, although they tried, no live penguins made it back with the explorers.

Paul's Injury

After completing his work with the penguins, Paul returned to studying seals. As taxidermist for the expedition, Paul's job was to collect skins and skulls from seals.

Early in November, Paul suffered a serious injury. Lifting a heavy frozen seal, Paul tore chest muscles near his left shoulder. Though immediately agonizing, the pain didn't worry Paul, who kept working despite discomfort. Unattended and untreated for several days, the damaged muscle remained painful.

Paul finally visited his lifesaver, Dr. Coman, who put his arm in a sling and instructed him not to use it until his chest muscles fully recovered. Paul had good intentions to follow the doctor's order, but time was slipping away. He had so much work to do before the expedition ended in three months.

At first Paul genuinely tried to work with one hand in the sling, but his struggle became a job all its own. Little by little he started cheating, using his forearm in the sling, pushing things with his elbow, finally slipping his arm out to lift, move, and, worst of all, carry heavy carcasses.

Paul should have recovered from his injury quickly. Because he had to use the damaged arm, Paul remained in his sling more than three months and did not fully recover until he received treatment after returning to New Zealand.

The Second Christmas

On the evening of December 25, 1929, Little America sparkled with creative splendor. Using only the resources available at their sparse camp, the explorers greeted the holiday with simplicity. As there were no "real" trees within thousands of miles, a makeshift artificial tree worked just fine for the men. Lacking traditional holiday decorations, they had to get creative, using the resources

143

that were on hand in the camp. Simple cotton adorned the tree along with chewing gum ornaments, cough drop lights, and cigarette wrapper tinsel. "Taffy" Davies, who had been Santa in Antarctica the previous year, again donned his Santa outfit as the men sang carols and enjoyed their memorable Christmas so far from home.

George Tennant planned for this day with his usual foresight. While a traditional turkey was unattainable, he had stashed the last salvageable chicken parts after the pups' earlier rampage. He decided that the occasional missing legs or stuffed gaps where wings had once been gave the entree an exotic look. Garnished with mountains of potatoes and vegetables, the crispy brown skin of the chicken pieces glistened as George placed his masterpiece on the table where the men were gathered. Even the men who weren't fond of chicken were impressed by George's presentation. Not even a few stray reindeer hairs diminished the beautiful and delectable meal. This special celebration set Paul to wondering what his parents, sister Carrol, and best buddy Alton Lindsey were eating and doing back home.

Fifteen

Catastrophes on Water and Land

Antarctica
Summer 1930

Trapped at Sea

With the arrival of 1930, everyone began anticipating the voyage home. They never imagined that painful setbacks and losses from the sea and mountains would strike before they left Antarctica. While Paul and the men at the camp worked through January, they often thought about the crew members of the whaling ships in the Ross Sea, like those from the *C.A. Larsen* and the *Ross*, who were searching for whales and also trying to find a safe route through the pack ice for both themselves and the Byrd Expedition.

On board each ship were "chasers," small boats with a harpoon gun mounted on the bow. The chasers would be launched from the large whaling ship. When close to their quarry, the crew fired the harpoon into the whale. Attached to the harpoon was a stout line. The line was used to pull the massive dead whale aboard the whaling ship through large, extra-wide doors where it would then be processed in the "factory" aboard. Some of these giant mammals, such as the blue whales, weigh more than 300,000 pounds. Almost nothing went to waste. The crew cut up and froze the meat and melted the blubber in boilers where it was refined into whale oil and stored. Some of the products obtained from the whales were highly valued: oil for lamps and candles, glue, leather, and fertilizer. Even some of the bones were made into fashion products such as girdles. The men on board believed that the serious risks they faced each day were far outweighed by the final reward—the large amount of money they received for the dangerous effort.

The crews of the Norwegian chasers returned to their mother ships with discouraging reports. Due to weather and tide patterns in 1930, there was more ocean ice present than ever before, making the pack ice around the continent impassable. News went from bad to worse. Huge bergs were cornering and blocking the chasers/scouting vessels that went out ahead of the whaling ships. If the small chasers couldn't locate a clear path, the massive whaling ships wouldn't stand a chance.

Radio messages from the more determined scouting crews were frequent and often upsetting. One chaser tried to force its way through the pack ice but hit an iceberg and sank. Fortunately, the crew was rescued.

Dangers persisted. Another of the whaling ships, which had turned back toward safety even before its sister-ship lost a chaser, drifted into a treacherous region of the Ross Sea. The twelve-foot-thick frozen ice closed in around the sea, trapping it instantly. The ship could not move or withstand for long the immense pressure of freezing ice around its hull, potentially crushing the metal like a tin can. The men could do nothing but wait.

For days the captive crew watched, hoping for a shift in the ice or a crack to appear just wide enough to open

Camping on the trail (courtesy National Archives, College Park, Maryland).

a path toward freedom. One day passed. The watch continued. The second day lingered. Unless there was a break soon, the crew would have to survive a winter frozen in the ice.

This time the Antarctic Sea relented, opening a lead just wide enough for the vessel to squeeze through. With all extra hands leaning over the deck watching for openings, the men tensely guided their ship to safety.

News of her success lifted spirits at Little America, but the celebration was brief. As the sea opened for the sailors, the land crew was battling a mountain that had become a deadly foe.

Mountain Casualties

In the spring Dr. Gould had led his geological exploration team a grueling four hundred miles to the Queen Maud Range of mountains to study the terrain, gather samples, and get scientific data. They were especially interested in obtaining rock samples from the mountains to see if they matched the type found in Australia and South America. They found what they were looking for and now had the first definitive evidence that the three land masses of Australia, South America, and Antarctica had once been part of one large continent.

The men at Little America experienced the same concern for Gould's party as they had for the men trapped at sea. Communication was often lost. Delayed by storms and large fields of crevasses, the group was in a life-or-death struggle as food was running out. Through sheer determination, Gould led his party back from the Queen Maud Mountains safely after a difficult expedition that took almost three months. Radio contact resumed as they neared Little America. The message came through clearly. Although very low on supplies, all the men survived and would be back at camp soon.

The first glimpse of Gould's team appeared through the sun's midday glare on January 19. Tiny figures emerged over the horizon. One by one the figures popped up so much like the little Adélie penguins springing from the sea onto land, the observers at camp had to remind themselves that there was no water where they looked. As they came closer, the tiny figures, in furry silhouettes and strides that could not belong to penguins, assured those who watched that the approaching cluster really was Dr. Gould's party returning from their mountain expedition. As the explorers approached, everyone at camp felt relieved. The anxious hours of waiting were finally over.

Nearly every man stopped his work to welcome the Gould party home. The lucky explorers had somehow overcome yet another brush with tragedy. "Byrd luck" still thrived. Perhaps because they were now so near the end of their expedition, the men cherished this return more than any other.

By the time Paul set aside his taxidermy, the Gould party was just reaching camp and being met by the waiting men. Besides the men's voices, Paul heard the familiar barking of sledge dogs. Paul looked forward to seeing the survivors and his sledge dogs again. When he opened the door, his heart sank. A great many dogs were missing, including his trusty companions. Where was Pete? Paul knew what must have happened, but he held his questions until after the celebration.

It took him some time to ask Gould what happened. After all, he was grateful the men survived their ordeal,

Team on the go (courtesy National Archives, College Park, Maryland).

and he knew the sacrifices Antarctica sometimes demanded. Though he dreaded the awful details, he had to know about his dogs. Paul was painfully aware that Antarctica required decisions that were often difficult to make and even harder to understand. Paul, a lover of animals since childhood, held animals, in particular the expedition dogs, in high regard. Without the dog teams, their journey would surely fail, and the dogs were in that respect, equally as important as the men. Despite this knowledge, Paul was well aware that if a decision had to be made between human and animal, the animal would be the one sacrificed to save a human life. That still didn't make it any easier to accept for an animal lover like Paul who valued all living things.

When Paul finally got Gould off by himself, the compassionate geologist knew that the truth would be hard. So he began by telling Paul what a hero Pete had been.

In the region of the crevasses, he explained, the men knew any miscalculated step could send them all tumbling to our deaths. But Pete led the way. Like a radio signal, Pete raced ahead of the men, his instinct guiding them from one clear space to the next. He would cross dangerous gaps at right angles and, as a result, helped the men avoid falling into the crevasses.

But it was after the men passed through that region and became stranded that things went from bad to worse. The men began running out of supplies, so sacrifices had to be made, Gould told him.

Paul knew the harsh realities of Antarctic exploration. If stranded and low on food, the rule was to kill the weaker dogs and feed them to the stronger. Keeping the best dogs healthy on an expedition was as essential to surviving as making sure all the men were hearty enough to get everyone back safely. Without the dogs to pull the

151

Team on the trail, waiting for the signal to go (courtesy National Archives, College Park, Maryland).

Team resting on the trail (courtesy National Archives, College Park, Maryland).

sledges carrying the food and tents, everyone would perish. That meant that some of Paul's dogs would have perished then, but not Pete.

Then Gould continued, telling Paul that time lingered and things grew even worse. That meant killing some of the healthy dogs to preserve only the very best.

"But why Pete?" asked Paul.

Dr. Gould explained that though Pete was healthy, he was older. With so few dogs left and food scarce, they could only afford to keep the youngest and strongest.

Dr. Gould reiterated that Pete had helped them survive and credited Paul with training him well. In the end, Pete died a hero. Although he was proud of Pete's status for having saved the other dogs and getting the men back to camp safely, Paul was still troubled over the loss of his loyal companion and the decisions that had to be made. For him, this was his "unhappiest day at Little America." This memory would haunt Paul for years to come, and on his future journeys he would devise clever ways to save his admired canine adventurers.

Sixteen
The Expedition Ends

Little America, Antarctica
Summer 1930

Preparing for Home

Following the successful return of Dr. Gould's mountain expedition, the emotional tide turned once more. The men began to lose hope that they would be going home this year. News about the *Eleanor Bolling* and the *City of New York's* return to Antarctica to transport them home grew bleaker with every radio communication. Cruising along the edges of the almost solid ice pack, neither ship could find a safe passage through the ice. Never in the history of Antarctic exploration had the pack ice remained so thick in summer. After trying for an entire month to get through, the ships' captains had to change plans before both vessels were trapped without fuel. Soon the temperatures would drop, refreezing the pack ice and forcing the men to spend another winter in Little America.

With faint hope and barely any time left, the *Eleanor Bolling* gave over her coal supply to the *City of New York*, saving just enough to return to New Zealand to get more.

The *City of New York* continued, its crew searching for a way through the ice and hoping for an opening as time slipped away.

The men of Little America prepared for their departure in hopes that the *City of New York* would successfully reach them. They sorted equipment into three levels of importance. Category "A" materials were guaranteed space on the return trip. These included men and their personal belongings, scientific data, and the most valuable equipment borrowed for the expedition.

Expensive machinery and material of high value earned category "B" grade status. Extra food and emergency stores that could be transported only on the rare chance that storage room could be found on the ship were marked category "C." Finally, anything that had to be left behind—primarily the airplanes—was labeled as category "D."

Leaving the historic planes behind was unavoidable. With only one ship returning now to bring them home, there was simply no room for them. The men did what they could to preserve the aircraft. They anchored the planes in flying position with their skis down and secured them so they could one day be used by future explorers or be brought back to the states. Years later an expedition would find the *Floyd Bennett* preserved in good condition. Unfortunately, as they readied the historic plane for flight a crevasse opened under it and damaged it beyond repair. Sadly it was abandoned and eventually disappeared.

Transporting all the materials became the men's biggest concern. With the chance that the *City of New York* might arrive any day, the men moved supplies as quickly as possible. The ice on the side of the Bay where the men worked couldn't hold the weight of heavy equipment.

Small pressure ridges opened gaps in the ice, leaving the area unsafe for stacking supplies.

Seven miles west of Little America was Floyd Bennett Bay, an inlet with a sturdy coastline. The *City of New York* could dock there, quickly load, and set sail for New Zealand with every man aboard.

The dogs remaining on the expedition were back to work hauling equipment as they had in earlier days. Sledge by sledge, they dragged the category A, B, and C class supplies to a spot less than three quarters of a mile from the edge of the Bay.

Within days, the heaping cache of supplies stood ready for quick loading as many of the men waited impatiently for the ship to take them home. Even if the *City of New York* was able to reach Little America a handful of men, especially the scientists, began to entertain thoughts of extending their stay in Antarctica another full year. Among those men was Paul.

One Last Plea

The explorers who wanted to stay in Antarctica all had great intentions. Dr. Gould believed that an extra year of collecting data would add depth to his research. He especially wanted to collect more unique geological specimens to help explain how the Antarctic continent was formed. The meteorologists intended to double their body of work by adding another year of data. Paul wanted to continue his wildlife studies, focusing on long-term information about the penguins and seals. Each would be providing a unique contribution to scientific knowledge.

Paul and the scientists approached Commander Byrd together, hoping a unified plea would be more persuasive. In the end Byrd decided against allowing any member of the expedition to remain for another year. Byrd felt that their original goals had been met, and it would be too dangerous to remain. No men had been lost in their expedition thus far, and he didn't want to tempt fate by pressing his "Byrd luck."

Boarding the *City of New York*

Though chief radio operator Malcolm Hanson was expecting to hear the status of the ship for several days, the radio message transmitted early one morning in mid-February still surprised him. With the aid of a powerful wind at her stern, the *City of New York* was pressing through the pack. But the journey was treacherous and the end result still uncertain.

Every natural element conspired against the ship. Because black, overcast skies blocked the sun, the crew was unable to use a sextant to establish its position. So near the South Magnetic Pole, the ship's compass was inaccurate. With little visibility and the inaccurate compass, Captain Melville and his crew could only roughly estimate the ship's position. With the *City of New York* potentially off course by many miles, the ship slowly felt its way through the ice.

A Ross Sea storm suddenly rocked the ship. Conditions worsened. Temperatures dropped as the wind gusts swirled in excess of one hundred miles per hour. Waves that earlier had tossed the ship about were now replaced by sprays of water that froze on her decks and anywhere else it landed. The ship was in danger of sinking under the crushing weight of 200 tons of ice coating her decks and rigging.

As Captain Melville and the officers steered the ship, the crew frantically chipped away at cakes of ice that covered the vessel. Then, without warning, the sky cleared enough to reveal a shocking sight. Unable to navigate accurately, the *City of New York* was over 300 miles off course and about to run aground on Ross Island. Decisiveness and quick reflexes saved them. Melville directed the ship around the northern edge of the island, and with the ship's position established they headed toward Little America.

The *City of New York* sighted the Barrier ice at the eastern end of Ross Island and sailed alongside the wall of ice to the east until crossing Discovery Inlet only one hundred miles from where the explorers waited. It looked as if the expedition could attempt a return home.

Byrd gave the orders to break camp. The men sledged the last of the personal equipment across the Barrier and added them to the mountainous cache. The radio station made its last broadcast and was silenced forever. Each man was allowed to return with only one duffel bag of personal belongings and whatever he could carry to the ship on his back. Space on the return trip would be scarce. Groups of two or three men started their final trek across the Bay. Turning to take a last look at Little America, the joy of returning to civilization was mixed with the sadness of leaving their Antarctic home. Emotions ran deep. They knew very few would ever return to this harsh and exotic continent.

Paul wasn't among the first groups to leave Little America and board the *City of New York*. He worked late at the base camp, completing last minute projects. In truth, he was stalling. Despite missing his family, he hated to leave. Finally, he closed up his work area and plodded across the Bay of Whales. The soft crunching

One last look at Little America (courtesy Byrd Polar Research Center Archival Program, The Ohio State University Libraries, #7801–15).

underfoot echoed solemnly in the frozen silence. As he plodded along in the thick snow, Paul reflected upon his journey, reaffirming to himself that it was indeed his honor to be a part of something so magnificent as this expedition.

At Floyd Bennett Bay, only the towering masts and upper sails of the *City of New York* were visible above a fog bank as she slowly rounded the West Cape. Once she was securely anchored, the men loaded her quickly. Immediately the water around the ship began filling with ice that could trap the ship. For eighteen hours the men loaded supplies into every nook of the *City of New York*.

Though one arm was still in a sling, Paul helped as much as he could. All the while, he doubted that everything would fit on only one ship. Unable to manage them with one hand, Paul let Quin Blackburn take care of his seven sisters' dog team.

The last two dog teams from Little America carried Commander Byrd and radio operator Howard Mason to the ship. Mason, ill from an appendicitis attack, had been in bed throughout the last weeks of the expedition.

Everyone was concerned about Mason. Throughout the expedition, they had lost no human lives. After ship accidents, sub-zero storms, and disappearances in blizzards, the men had fought too hard to let one of their own die from a ruptured appendix. To everyone's relief, Mason was carried onto the *City of New York* where he would survive the trip to the hospital and fully recover at their first port in New Zealand.

The Final Sacrifice

Yet not every living creature on the expedition would return home. At the last moments on the continent, Antarctica would claim more lives.

With only one ship to carry everyone, the truth became apparent. There would be no room on this ship for many of the dogs, including Paul's. Only sixty of "the best" dogs were taken on board, a fact that Paul and the other men finally accepted as an unavoidable necessity. Although Paul grieved for the dogs that gave their lives, he understood and appreciated the sacrifice they made on behalf of their human companions. This was yet another personal reminder to Paul about Antarctica's harsh environment that claims so much from so many. He silently made a solemn promise to honor the memories of the dogs left behind on this unforgiving continent and vowed he would never forget their heroic spirit.

A Passion for Life

On February 19, 1930, Captain Melville gave the order to cast off at 9:30 in the morning. With all hands on board and anchor lines lifted, the *City of New York* inched away from land. Thin layers of ice crunched on either side as she crept into the open Bay, moving slowly through the ice in the Bay of Whales, heading for Discovery Inlet. The men, filled with mixed emotions, took their last look at Little America.

Byrd summoned everyone on deck. The *City* had brought over a year's worth of mail and gifts such as fruitcakes from home. The men were eager to read their letters. Byrd told the assembled group that work duties would not resume for twenty-four hours. They had a full day to relax and read their big piles of mail.

Paul's old bunk in the forecastle was waiting for him. Clutching a stack of family mail, Paul stepped to the edge of the deck for another look at the Barrier. Though he would soon be reunited with his family, Paul knew his passion for life would thrive on the frozen plateau of his Antarctic home. The white desolation and solitude was now a part of him. As the towering ice cliffs disappeared over the horizon, they weren't receding into Paul's past. He realized they were beckoning him to return; yet, he still didn't know what life had in store for him. His first expedition was ending with many successful milestones recorded, but little did he know that he would return again and again. For the "Eagle on Ice," the next adventure was just beyond the horizon.

Major Accomplishments of Byrd's First Expedition

Byrd (with pilot Balchen, pilot/radio operator June, and aerial photographer McKinley) flew the historic first flight over the South Pole.

The expedition moved Antarctic exploration from the "Heroic Age" to the "Mechanical Age." Byrd "proved that airplanes, radio communication, and motorized transport could be used in Antarctica to advance exploration and science."

The expedition mapped thousands of miles of unknown territories.

Byrd, using aircraft to explore, discovered the mountain ranges he named the Ford and Rockefeller Mountains.

Gould and his party spent almost three months exploring the geological history in the Queen Maud Mountains.

Gould's party claimed land east of the 150th meridian as part of Marie Byrd Land for the United States.

Gould found sandstone rock that would link the continents of Australia, South America, and Antarctica as having been joined long ago as a single land mass.

Through photographs and motion pictures the world's people were able to see the images of the previously unexplored areas of Antarctica.

The expedition collected vital scientific data on wildlife, plants, weather, and magnetic observations.

The expedition brought back specimens of several penguin species (mounted by Siple) for the American Museum of Natural History in New York City.

Epilogue

Washington, D.C.
March 28, 1958

Award-winning Achievements

In 1958, the National Geographic Society bestowed its highest honor for exploration, the Hubbard Medal, to Antarctic explorer Paul Allman Siple. For a tribute so unique and distinguished, Earl Warren, Chief Justice of the Supreme Court, was invited to make the formal presentation. Only the seventeenth person to receive this prestigious award since it was first given in 1906, Paul's reputation is now permanently linked with the most respected explorers in history. Robert Peary, first to reach the North Pole and Roald Amundsen, first to reach the South Pole, as well as noted Antarctic explorer Sir Ernest Shackleton are all previous Hubbard recipients. Even Paul's mentor and friend Admiral Richard E. Byrd, leader of the Antarctic expeditions and the first man to fly over both the North and South Poles, is included among this elite list of medal winners.

The inscription on Paul's medal reads:

THE HUBBARD MEDAL

AWARDED TO

PAUL A. SIPLE

WHOSE BOLD ANTARCTIC
EXPLORATIONS AND RESEARCHES
SPANNING THIRTY YEARS
HAVE BROADENED THE HORIZONS
OF GEOGRAPHIC KNOWLEDGE

SCIENTIFIC LEADER OF THE
FIRST GROUP TO WINTER AT THE
SOUTH POLE, 1957

March 28, 1958

During the medal ceremony tribute, Chief Justice Warren noted: "Our Hubbard medalist today is of the same stature as the great explorers I have mentioned. Six times he has journeyed to the forbidden continent of Antarctica, the first time with Admiral Byrd as a young Eagle Scout." This first journey changed him from a Scout with boyhood dreams to a man who made historic contributions to science and exploration.

Later he visited the continent as "scientific leader of the first group of men ever to winter at the South Pole" where he survived during "the longest, darkest, and coldest winter yet endured by man." Chief Justice Warren

Paul Siple on the cover of *Time* magazine (courtesy Siple Family Collection).

went on to say that the medal was "for his extraordinary feat, for the increases he has made in geographic knowledge, and for his superb leadership in the International Geophysical Year."

Sometimes referred to as "the Nation's Mr. Antarctica," Dr. Siple made many other impressive contributions to science. Leading this list of achievements is his doctoral research into weather and climates. He expanded the world's understanding of weather by coining the term "wind chill" and deriving and indexing a formula for determining wind chill factor, which meteorologists still use today.

A Hubbard Medal Ceremony Surprise

Chief Justice Warren also talked about Paul's love of dogs. Paul remembered the dogs that served the men so well but had to be sacrificed on that first expedition. Paul said at the time, "I am sure that the loss of my dogs will always be one of the saddest experiences of my life." Over the years Paul's love for animals never diminished. He went to great efforts to save them on his subsequent Antarctic trips. Most recently in 1957, when he was Scientific Leader at the South Pole Station he intervened to try to save an Antarctic-born malamute-husky named Bravo, the only dog at the station. At the end of the expedition, the Navy listed Bravo as surplus property. Paul had to return home before he found out Bravo's fate.

Chief Justice Warren mentioned that Paul's concern for dogs "indicates one of the qualities which has so endeared him to all his associates in the years of brilliant Antarctic exploration." Warren called Paul forward to receive his medal. At that moment, Paul had no idea that the committee had one more surprise in store for the Antarctic hero. Paul accepted the Hubbard Medal with characteristic humility. Referring to his time in Antarctica, Paul said, "A man isn't out there by himself doing a job. He is surrounded literally by thousands of people . . . backing up the expedition, people back home, the men beside him. It is impossible to single out any one man. On behalf of all those," Paul concluded, "who have been taking part in the exploration and uncovering of a continent, I humbly express my thanks."

After the medal presentation, Lieutenant John Tuck, Jr. stepped into the room. Tuck, who had commanded military personnel at the South Pole Station, also loved dogs and worked with them in Antarctica. At his side stood Bravo.

Seeing Bravo, Paul's face lit up, his brown eyes twinkling. Unlike many of his dogs from that first expedition with Commander Byrd, Bravo had made it home safely.

Tuck announced that Paul's efforts to save Bravo, "the first dog to winter at the South Pole," from being sold as surplus property worked. At Paul's unusual request, the Navy proclaimed Bravo a V.I.D.—a Very Important Dog. With Bravo's new military status, he received an honorable discharge and was placed under the orders of Lieutenant Tuck. Bravo symbolized the gentle spirit of all the dogs lost on Paul's first expedition.

It was a fitting end to Paul's medal ceremony. This time without demanding anything in return, Antarctica honored Paul and the dogs whose sacrifice had made so much possible. For the "Eagle on Ice," life's next adventure was waiting.

Appendices

Chronology of Paul Allman Siple

1908	Born in Montpelier, Ohio on December 18 to Clyde L. Siple and Fannie Hope (Allman) Siple
1918	Moved with family to Erie, Pennsylvania (April)
1920	Joined Boy Scout Troop No. 24
1923	Earned Eagle Scout rank and joined Sea Scouts, attaining rank of Able Sea Scout (eventually became "Mate" of the Sea Scout ship *Niagara* on his 21st birthday)
1920–28	Earned 59 merit badges at time of application in July 1928 for Byrd Antarctic Expedition (this was nearly all the badges available at that time, and eventually he earned 61 badges)
1926	Graduated from Erie's Central High School in June
1926–27	Worked as assistant draftsman with Pennsylvania State Highway Department to earn money for college
1927–28	Freshman year at Allegheny College in Meadville, Pennsylvania
1928	Selected in a nationwide competition as the Boy Scout to accompany USN Commander Richard E. Byrd on the first Byrd Antarctic Expedition (August)
1928–30	Departed from New York Harbor on *City of New York* on first Byrd Antarctic Expedition (August 25, 1928) Selected by Byrd to winter-over in Antarctica Worked as naturalist, dog team driver, and taxidermist, and collected specimens (skins) of seals, penguins, and flying birds for the American Museum of Natural History in New York City Returned June 1930
1930–32	Returned to Allegheny College in Meadville, Pennsylvania (September 1930), completing his last three years in two years, graduating in June 1932 with a Bachelor of Science degree in Biology (minor in Geology)

1930–33	Lectured on tours (sometimes with Admiral Byrd) to Councils of Boy Scouts of America and other service groups
1931	Published *Boy Scout with Byrd* (Putnam)
1932	Published *Exploring at Home* (Putnam)
1932–33	Backpacked on "world" tour to England, Europe (including Russia), Asia Minor, and North Africa
1933	Selected to go on Byrd Antarctic Expedition II
	Assisted Admiral Byrd in planning and preparations for the expedition
1933–35	Byrd Antarctic Expedition II:
	Member of Byrd's personal staff
	Acted as Chief Biologist
	Leader of Marie Byrd Land Sledging Party, collecting lichens and mosses and mapping 30,000 square miles of new territory
1935	Identified and cataloged the lichens and mosses collected on BAE II, finding 84 new species of lichens and 5 new species of mosses (published material in *Annals of the Missouri Botanical Garden*, vol. 25, April 1938)
1935–36	Hundreds of lectures to scientific and public service groups, colleges, schools, and Boy Scout audiences in the U.S.
1936	Published *Scout to Explorer* (Putnam)
1936	Enrolled in graduate program at Clark University in Worcester, Massachusetts, specializing in Geography and the study of "the effects of geographical conditions on humans and their possessions" (September)
1936	Married Ruth Ida Johannesmeyer on December 29th
1939	Attained Ph.D. in Geography and Climatology from Clark University in Worcester, Massachusetts
	Dissertation entitled: *Adaptations of the Explorer to the Climate of Antarctica* (June)

1939–41   United States Antarctic Service Expedition:
           Assistant to Admiral Richard E. Byrd
           Supervisor of supplies and equipment and responsi-
           ble for all expedition logistics
           Senior geographer
           Leader of West Base, Little America III, Bay of
           Whales
           Served as navigator on all Antarctic exploratory
           flights
           Conducted experiments (with Charles Passel) which
           resulted in the devising of the formula for the wind
           chill index (published in *Proceedings of the American
           Philosophical Society*, vol. 89, 1945)
1940–46   Three daughters born: Ann Byrd, June 6, 1940; Jane
           Paulette, October 11, 1942; Mary Cathrin, October
           26, 1946
1941–42   Employed by U.S. Army as civilian expert on design
           of cold climate clothing and equipment and as head
           of research and map projects
           Commissioned as captain in U.S. Army (July 1942)
1941–45   During World War II, serving as military geogra-
           pher for U.S. Army Quartermaster Corps, he ad-
           vised the government on, and directed research on,
           clothing and environmental protection of troops in
           all climates; organized the U.S. Quartermaster
           Corps' Climate Research Laboratory; and was re-
           sponsible for the initiation of new design of cold
           weather gear (especially the cold weather parka and
           thermal-barrier boot) for all of which he was
           awarded the Legion of Merit medal
1945–46   Traveled to Arctic and Greenland for observation
           and research, as this area was of interest to national
           defense with the onset of the Cold War
1946–47   At Little America IV, Antarctica, as Scientific and
           Polar Advisor and Senior Representative of U.S.
           War Dept. on a naval operation called *United States*

Navy Antarctic Development Program (AKA *Operation High Jump*) (December 1946–April 1947)

1946–53   Discharged from military as Lieutenant Colonel (August 1946)

Joined U.S. Army General Staff in civilian capacity as military geographer and science adviser for research and development, directing the Army's environmental research program, eventually becoming a specialist in polar, mountain, desert, and tropical climates

1947   Received Boy Scouts of America Silver Buffalo Award, ("for distinguished service to boyhood") (May 28, 1947)

1950–53   During Korean War, again studied winter combat problems and traveled to the battle lines twice to observe the effectiveness of newly designed military clothing

1953–55   Director of Scientific Projects and Environmental Living for USN Task Force 43, in preparation for Operation Deep Freeze I (which would set up in Antarctica, among other programs, McMurdo Station as a support base for the South Pole station and Little America V as support base for Byrd Station), all of which was preparation for Deep Freeze II, IGY (International Geophysical Year, to run from July 1957 to December 1958—a year in which 67 countries would conduct coordinated research worldwide, including 11 nations manning 40 stations in Antarctica)

1955–56   Operation Deep Freeze I (in Antarctica):
Deputy to Admiral Byrd, Director of U.S. Antarctic Programs
Scientific Adviser for Deep Freeze I

1956   Appeared on the cover of *Time* magazine (December 31, 1956), the article covering the anticipated first winter that men would experience the 6 months of complete darkness (from March 22 to September 22) at the South Pole

1956–57 Deep Freeze II, IGY, and initial year of operation of the U.S. IGY Geographical South Pole Station (Amundsen-Scott Station):
Scientific Leader of the Amundsen-Scott South Pole Station during IGY—this was the first group to winter-over at the South Pole, a group of 18 men who would be the first to experience the six months of the blustery sub-zero sunless South Polar night

1957–58 *National Geographic Magazine* featured articles by Paul Siple about that first IGY South Pole experience (July 1957 and April 1958)

1957–60 Received, for his leadership role in the heroic and successful first wintering at the South Pole, *National Geographic's* Hubbard Medal (March)—also medals from the U.S. Army, U.S. Defense Department, three other Geographical societies, five of his seven honorary doctorate degrees, and more, for this accomplishment

1958 Awarded the "National Distinguished Service Award, Order of the Arrow, Boy Scouts of America" (highest award for distinguished service) (May 17, 1958)

1958–63 Scientific adviser, U.S. Army Research Office, continuing environmental research

1959 Published *90 Degrees South* (Putnam)

1961 Awarded American Specialist Grant by State Department for a three-month goodwill trip to Australia, New Zealand, Antarctica, and India under the Department's cultural exchange program

1963–66 Served as the first Scientific Attaché to the U.S. Embassies in Canberra, Australia and Wellington, New Zealand

1966 Suffered a stroke while in Wellington, New Zealand (June 6) and returned home to Virginia (September)

1966	Returned to work with Army Research and Development as Special Scientific Adviser (November)
1968	Died of a heart attack at his office desk in Arlington, Virginia, November 25

Additional Honors
(Partial List)

Seven honorary doctorate degrees

Medals from five geographical societies (three American and two international)

Three Congressional Byrd Antarctic Expedition Medals

Legion of Merit (1946)

Honorary M.B.E. (Order of the British Empire, 1946)

Decoration for Exceptional Civilian Service, Department of the Army (December 1957)

Distinguished Service Award, Department of Defense (April 1958)

Superior Honor Award, Department of State (December 1966)

Paul A. Siple Award, a silver medallion to be awarded biennially for excellence in basic research, to a U.S. Army in-house laboratory scientist or a team of researchers

Antarctic landmarks named for him: Mount Siple, Siple Island, Siple Ridge, Siple Coast (New Zealand), and Siple Station

Men on Byrd's Expedition Who Wintered-Over (Little America I)

Commander Richard Evelyn Byrd

Claire (Alex) Alexander (tailor who made polar clothing; wood carver)

Bernt Balchen (chief pilot; Norwegian craftsman who made sledges)

George Hamilton (Blackie) Black (supply officer)

Quin Blackburn (surveyor)

Christoffer (Chris) Braathen (Norwegian ski expert and dog driver)

Kennard Bubier (Marine Corps sergeant)

Jack Bursey (dog driver)

Arnold Clark (cook's helper)

Dr. Francis Coman (expedition physician)

Freddie Crockett (dog driver)

Victor Czegka (machinist)

Frank (Taffy) Davies (physicist)

Pete Demas (airplane mechanic)

Joe de Ganahl (radio operator)

Jim Feury (Irish surveyor)

Edward (Eddie) Goodale (dog driver)

Charles "Chips" Gould (carpenter)

Laurence (Larry) Gould (geologist)

Bill (Cyclone) Haines (meteorologist)

Malcolm Hanson (chief radio operator)

Henry Harrison, Jr. (meteorologist)

Harold June (pilot)

Charles Lofgren (Byrd's personal secretary)

Howard Mason (radio operator)

Captain Ashley McKinley (aerial photographer)

Thomas "Tom" Mulroy (In charge of kerosene, oil, and gasoline)

John "Jack" O'Brien (Irish surveyor)

Russell Owen (*New York Times* reporter; librarian)

Captain Alton Parker (Marine Corps; pilot)

Carl Petersen (radio operator)
Martin Ronne (tailor; sail maker)
Benjamin "Benny" Roth (U.S. Army Sergeant)
Joe Rucker (Paramount movie man)
Paul Siple (taxidermist, dog driver)
Dean Smith (pilot)
Sverre Strom (Norwegian craftsman who made sledges)
George Tennant (chief cook)
Mike Thorne (surveyor)
Willard Van der Veer (Paramount movie man)
Norman Vaughn (dog driver)
Arthur Walden (head dog driver)

In the Footsteps of Paul Siple:
Antarctic Scout Program,
Boy Scouts of America

The Antarctic Scout program began in 1928 when Eagle Scout Paul Siple was selected from thousands of applicants in a nationwide competition with other Boy Scouts to accompany Commander Richard Byrd on his expedition to Antarctica. In 1958 Dr. Paul Siple asked the National Council of the Boy Scouts of America to select an Eagle Scout to accompany him to the South Pole. The first Eagle Scout selected was Richard Chappell. Since 1958, based on available funding by the National Science Foundation in conjunction with the Boy Scouts of America, other Eagle Scouts have been selected to go to Antarctica. While there they work with scientists and conduct research during the expeditions scheduled during the Antarctic summer season.

For more information on the Antarctic Scout Program visit the Boy Scouts of America National Council website, and search the *U.S. Antarctic Program*.

Boy Scouts of America National Council: http://www.scouting.org

Boy Scouts Who Continued
in the Footsteps of Paul Siple

Paul Allman Siple. Ph.D. (1928)
Erie, Pennsylvania

Richard L. Chappell, Ph.D. (1957)
New York, New York

Mark W. Leinmiller (1978)
Atlanta, Georgia

Douglas C. Barnhart, M.D. (1984)
Hoover, Alabama

Louis P. Sugarman (1986)
Farmington Hills, Michigan

Robert Scot Duncan (1989)
Irondale, Alabama

Tobermory (Toby) Ramulf Ovod-Everett (1992)
Anchorage, Alaska

Ernst Kass Kastning IV (1995)
Haymarket, Virginia

Benjamin Joseph Hasse (1998)
Iron Mountain, Michigan

Timothy Ian Brox (2001)
Fresno, California

Bradford A. Range (2003)
Marietta, Georgia

Benjamin J. Pope (2005)
Newton, Massachusetts

Facts About Antarctica Today

- Fifth largest of the seven continents (1.5 times the size of the United States)
- Surface area of over five million square miles which is double in size during the winter
- World's coldest, windiest, driest, iciest, and highest continent
- Surrounded by the Southern Ocean
- No permanent residents, only personnel at research stations
- Roughly circular in shape with two large indentations—Ross and Weddell Seas
- Over 90 percent of the continent covered by Antarctic ice sheets containing 70 percent of the world's fresh water
- Ross Ice Shelf is the size of France and produces the world's largest icebergs
- Coldest temperature of −128.6 F. on July 21, 1983 at Russian Vostok station
- Highest winds of 199 m.p.h. recorded at Dumont d'Urville Base Station in July 1972
- Highest elevation is Vinson Massif at 16,067 feet
- Average elevation of 7500 feet
- Continent defined as a desert with less than ten inches average annual precipitation.
- Plant life limited to mostly lichens and mosses
- Governed by the Antarctic Treaty

Sources:

CIA-World Factbook: http://www.cia.gov/library/publications/the-world-factbook/geos/ay.html
World Book Encyclopedia: www.worldbook.com

Glossary

Glossary

Adélie penguin	Black and white markings distinguish this common Antarctic medium-size penguin
Albatross	A large oceanic bird that returns to land only to raise their young; some species have wingspans as wide as eleven feet
Aurora	Colored arches and streams of light in the night sky caused by electrical disturbances in the atmosphere
Barrier	In Antarctica the term references the Ross Ice Shelf
Barrier ice	Ice formations around the Antarctic continent in the winter that shrinks and breaks up in the summer
Bulkhead	The vertical partition between compartments on a boat; in a house it would be called a wall
Cache	A storage area for valuable supplies
Calving	Ice that splits and sheds off a glacier and falls into the water of a lake or ocean
Chasers	Small ships with a harpoon on the bow that chase and harpoon whales; carried aboard huge whaling ships
Crabeater seal	The world's most abundant seal; despite its name its primary food is not crabs but krill which it strains from the

	water through its specially shaped teeth
Emperor penguin	Black sides and white fronts with purple-edged bills are distinguishing markings of the largest of the penguins that are almost four-feet tall and 70–88 pounds
Equator	An imaginary circle around the earth that is equal distance from the North and South Poles; divides the earth's surface into Northern and Southern hemispheres
Euphausia	An extremely abundant shrimp-like type of krill about two inches long that is the basis for sustaining larger animal life such as seals, whales, and penguins
Factory ship	A whaling ship that processes the whales which are harpooned and caught
Forecastle	The front of a ship that contains the anchors
Frostbite	Freezing or partial freezing of skin due to exposure to cold air
Geographic South Pole	Most southern part of the earth
Ice dock	A flat shelf of ice that is thick enough to allow off loading of supplies from a ship
Ice floe	A sheet of ice that is floating on water
Ice pack	Floating pieces of ice driven by winds or current into a nearly continuous collection of ice
Iceberg	A large floating block of ice that has split off into the ocean from a glacier; only 1/8 of an iceberg is above the water, the other 7/8 is under the water

International Date Line (IDL)	The 180th meridian established as the place where each calendar day begins
Killer whale	Also known as an "orca" Largest of the dolphin family, this top predator feeds on other marine animals; as large as thirty feet in length with glossy black and white bodies
Krill	Planktonic organisms and larva that live in the oceans
Lead	An opening of water found in pack ice
Leopard seal	The only seal predator that eats warm blooded prey; diet includes penguins, young of other seals, krill, and fish; called sea leopards in earlier days
Magnetic South Pole	Southern magnetic pole of the earth's magnetic field; located hundreds of miles from the Geographic South Pole
Meteorologist	A person whose expertise is weather and weather forecasting
Mukluks	Waterproof boots made of animal skins that are large enough to be worn over shoes
Musher	A term for the driver of a dog sledge
Orca	See "killer whale"
Petrel	A sea bird often found far from land
Precipice	An overhang or steep drop-off
Ross Ice Shelf	A huge floating ice wall found in Antarctica's Ross Sea that is 100 to 200 feet above sea level and over 500 miles long; about the size of France
Sastrugi	Ridges of snow, created by the wind, that are parallel to wind direction and are usually a few inches high but can reach two to three feet
Scurvy	A disease caused by a lack of ascorbic acid that causes the teeth to loosen, or fall out, and bleeding under the skin

Sea Leopard	See leopard seal
Skua	A brownish predator seabird related to the seagull; common in the Antarctic
Sledge	A mode of transportation with runners for sliding, it is larger than a traditional sled and pulled by dogs whose energy moves it across the ice to carry supplies
Spy-hopping	A technique used by orca or killer whales where they rise out of the water vertically to look around the water's surface for prey
Topographer	A surveyor who measures relative positions and elevations of the earth's features to create maps and charts
Trimotor	A three-engine airplane
Weddell Seal	Mammal living the furthest south and reaching 900 pounds and ten feet in length with a diet consisting of fish, krill, and squid; remains near land year round
Whiteout	A cloudy condition over snow where there is no horizon or shadows; causes difficulty in determining the size and distance of objects
Windchill	The effect that wind speed has on how cold the air feels; increasing wind speed makes the apparent temperature lower

References

Sources for Quotes

Chapter One

Page 9: "In their holds and on . . . . . . unrelieved stay in the Antarctic," *Little America*, Byrd, page 3.

Page 11: "stating the reasons why he wishes to become a member of this expedition and why he feels he is qualified," *A Boy Scout With Byrd*, Siple, page 155.

Page 11: "Scouts in Race for Honor of Joining Byrd's Expedition," (newspaper headline), *The New York Times,* August 13, 1928.

Page 13: "scout's reason for applying," *A Boy Scout With Byrd*, Siple, page 156.

Page 15: "which two they themselves would choose . . . . . . send three Scouts on the expedition," *A Boy Scout With Byrd*, Siple, page 163.

Page 16: "Erie Scout With Byrd," (newspaper headline) *Erie Dispatch-Herald*, August 20, 1928.

Chapter Two

Page 17: "Byrd Ship to Sail Southward Today," (newspaper headline), *The New York Times*, August 25, 1928.

Page 18: "Boy Scouts Cheer as Siple Sails for Antarctic," (newspaper headline), *Erie Dispatch-Herald*, August 20, 1928.

Page 26: "He has two bunks already. If you want to get along as a sailor, you don't want to be bluffed so easily as that," *A Boy Scout With Byrd*, page 6.

Chapter Three

Page 28: "a humble servant and being recognized as a leader," Originally published in pamphlet, "Merit Badge Counseling," Boy Scouts of America, 1957. Reprint in Ministry of Scouting, National Association of United Methodist Scouters, no page numbers.

Page 33: "First-time . . . equator," *A Boy Scout With Byrd*, Siple, page 10.

Page 33: "All that has been written about the beauty of the South Sea Islands is no exaggeration," *A Boy Scout With Byrd*, Siple, page 16.

Page 34: "spiny sea urchins . . . in the least," *A Boy Scout With Byrd*, Siple, page 16.

Page 34: "tiny fish more . . . were feeding," *A Boy Scout With Byrd*, Siple, page 16.

Page 34: "Make the upper topsail fast," *A Boy Scout With Byrd*, Siple, page 19.

Page 35: "one hand for the ship and one for yourself," *A Boy Scout With Byrd*, Siple, page 38.

Page 38: "What a boon this tow . . . is to us. Without it we should be at a . . . through the ice," *Little America*, Carter, pages 58–59.

Page 39: "Everything . . . beginning to assume a gray sameness," *A Boy Scout With Byrd*, Siple, page 38.

Page 40: "I've never seen an unbeautiful iceberg," *Little America*, Carter, page 57.

Page 40: "beautiful ghosts of the Antarctic," *A Boy Scout With Byrd*, Siple, page 133.

Chapter Four

Page 44: "The thing we had come so far to see . . . as far as the eye could see . . . but there it was—the mysterious Barrier," *Little America*, Byrd, page 77.

Page 44: "a white cliff rising a hundred feet or more in defiance to keep us from going further south," *A Boy Scout With Byrd*, Siple, page 29.

Pages 45–48: "We stood silent as they came . . . They started to file away . . . in which they had come," *A Boy Scout With Byrd,* Siple, pages 30–31.

Page 53: "killller whales aroused dread . . . cutting the water," *Little America,* Byrd, page 100.

Chapter Six

Page 68: "the greatest craftsman in polar clothing," *Little America*, Byrd, page 22.

Chapter Nine

Page 92: "individual isolation was . . . . . . in Little America," *Little America,* Carter, page 84.

Chapter Eleven

Page 117: "like a white oak leaf . . . . . . strained out of the water," *A Boy Scout With Byrd*, Siple, pages 120–121.

Page 118: "The agile . . . . . . as he went," *A Boy Scout With Byrd*, Siple, page 121.

Chapter Twelve

Page 122: "wildest ride I ever had," *Little America*, Byrd, page 286.

Chapter Thirteen

Page 124: "Unchanged . . . . . . anywhere," *Little America*, Byrd, page 326.

Page 124: "If you . . . . . . as good as this," *Little America*, Byrd, page 326.

Page 128: "some of the men . . . . . . then," *Little America*, Byrd, pages 311–312.

Page 130: "Harold, ... overboard," *Little America*, Byrd, page 335.

Page 131: "Shall I do it, Commander?" *Little America*, Carter, page 126.

Page 131: "More!" *Little America*, Byrd, page 336.

Page 132: "My calculations. . . . Byrd," *Little America*, Byrd, page 341.

Page 133: "What was the Pole like?" *Little America*, Carter, page 129.

Page 133: "A white desolation and solitude," *Little America*, Carter, page 129.

Chapter Fifteen

Page 154: "unhappiest day at Little America," *Little America,* Carter, page 152.

Epilogue

Pages 166: "Our Hubbard Medalist . . . as a young Eagle Scout," *National Geographic Magazine*, June 1958, page 793.

Page 166: "scientific leader of the first group to winter at the South Pole," *National Geographic Magazine*, June 1958, page 792.

Page 166: "the longest . . . winter yet endured by man," *National Geographic Magazine*, June 1958, page 792.

Page 168: "for his extraordinary feat . . . leadership in the International Geophysical Year," *National Geographic Magazine*, June 1958, page 792.

Page 168: "the Nation's Mr. Antarctica," *National Geographic Magazine*, June 1958, page 792.

Page 168: "I am sure . . . saddest experiences of my life," *A Boy Scout With Byrd*, page 138.

Page 168: "indicates one of . . . exploration," *National Geographic Magazine*, June 1958, page 793.

Page 169: "A man isn't out there . . . impossible to single out any one man," *National Geographic Magazine*, June 1958, page 793.

Page 169: "On behalf . . . thanks," *National Geographic Magazine*, June 1958, page 793.

Page 169: "the first dog to winter at the South Pole," *National Geographic Magazine*, June 1958, page 792.

Sources for Figures

Chapter One

Page 7: Expedition Job Opportunities
Sources: Carter's *Little America*, pages 42–46; *Little America*, Byrd, pages 37–38.
Page 10: A Sampling of Expedition Supplies
Source: *Little America*, Carter, pages 38–39.
Page 13: Paul Siple's Scout Badges Related to the Needs of the Expedition
Source: *A Boy Scout With Byrd*, Siple, page 154.
Page 14: Boy Scout Finalists
Source: *A Boy Scout With Byrd*, Siple, page 159.

Chapter Two

Page 23: Ships in the Byrd Antarctic Expedition
Sources: *Little America*, Byrd, pages 37–38; *Little America*, Carter, pages 48–49.

Chapter Three

Page 39: Seasons In Northern and Southern Hemispheres
Source: *In Little America with Byrd*, Joe and Ola Hill, page 91.

Chapter Five

Page 60: Paul's Dog Team
Source: *A Boy Scout With Byrd*, Siple, photo insert between pages 50–51.

Chapter Nine

Page 89: Temperatures Recorded in Little America
Source: *Little America*, Byrd, page 39.
Page 90: Little America Daily Schedule
Sources: Byrd's *Little America*, pages 199–206; Carter's *Little America*, pages 89–97; *A Boy Scout With Byrd*, Siple, pages 85–92.
Page 94: Antarctic University Course Overview
Sources: *Little America*, Carter page 94; *A Boy Scout With Byrd*, Siple, page 91.
Page 97: Little America Menu
Sources: *Little America*, Byrd, pages 199–200 and 205–206; *A Boy Scout With Byrd*, Siple, page 102.

Chapter Ten

Page 109: Paul's New Dog Team
Source: *A Boy Scout With Byrd*, Siple, pages 102–103.

Chapter Sixteen

Page 163: Major Accomplishments of Byrd's First Expedition
Sources: *Little America,* Byrd*; Little America,* Carter; Byrd Papers:
http://library.osu.edu/sites/exhibits/byrdflight/legacy.html

Epilogue

Page 166: "The Hubbard Medal Awarded to Paul A. Siple"
Source: *National Geographic Magazine*, June 1958, page 792 (inscription on medal).

Resources Consulted

Books

Byrd, Richard E. *Discovery*. New York: G.P. Putnam's Sons, 1935.

———. *Little America*. New York: G.P. Putnam's Sons, 1930.

———. *Skyward*. New York: G.P. Putnam's Sons, 1928.

Carter, Paul A. *Little America: Town at the End of the World*. New York: Columbia University Press, 1979.

Goerler, Raimund E., ed. *To the Pole: The Diary and Notebook of Richard E. Byrd, 1925–1927*. Columbus, Ohio: Ohio State University Press, 1998.

Gould, Laurence McKinley. *COLD: The Record of An Antarctic Sledge Journey*. New York: Brewer, Warren, & Putnam, 1931.

Hill, Joe Jr., and Ola Davis Hill. *In Little America With Byrd*. Boston: Ginn and Company, 1937.

Leatherwood, Stephen and Randall Reeves. *Handbook of Whales and Dolphins*. Sierra Club Books, 1983.

Owen, Russell. *South of the Sun*. New York: John Day, 1934.

Pyne, Stephen. *The Ice: A Journey to Antarctica*. New York: Ballantine Books, 1988.

Siple, Paul. *A Boy Scout with Byrd*. New York: G.P. Putnam's Sons, 1931.

———. *Exploring at Home*. New York: G.P. Putnam's Sons, 1932.

———. *90 Degrees South*. New York: G.P. Putnam's Sons, 1959.

———. *Scout to Explorer*. New York: G.P. Putnam's Sons, 1936.

Sitwell, Nigel and Tom Ritchie. *Antarctic Primer*. Darien, Connecticut: Quark Expeditions, 1997.

Soper, Tony. *Antarctica: A Guide to Wildlife*. Old Saybrook, Connecticut: Globe Pequot Press, 1994.

Todd, Frank S. *Birds and Mammals of the Antarctic, Subantarctic & Falkland Islands*. Temecula, California: Ibis Publishing Company, 2004.

Vaughan, Norman D. *With Byrd at the Bottom of the World*. Harrisburg, Pennsylvania: Stackpole Books, 1990.

Watson, George E. *Birds of the Antarctic and Subantarctic*. Washington: American Geophysical Union, 1988.

Magazines, Journals, Brochures, Pamphlets

Anderson, Evelyn. "From Erie Eagle Scout to Polar Popularity," *Sunday: The Magazine of the Times-News*, November 25, 1990, pages 6–K, 7–K, 8–K.

"Antarctic Scientist Honored by The Society." *The National Geographic Magazine*, June, 1958, pages 792–793.

"From Maywood and Main to Marie Byrd Land." *Clark Now: The Magazine of Clark University*, vol. 9, no. 4, (fall 1980), pages 2–6.

Lynch, Joseph L. (Jr.). "A Scout's Journeys Remembered." *Sossi Journal,* November/December, 1996, pages 7–16.

Madden, Michael. "From the South Pole to South Main." *Worcester Magazine*, January 28, 1998.

"Montpelier Native Shivered to Fame." *The Fort Wayne Journal-Gazette*, January 13, 1985, no page number given.

"Paul Allman Siple." *Annals of the Association of American Geographers*. Vol. 59, no. 4 (December 1969), pages 815–819

"Paul Allman Siple" (obituary). *Polar Record*, Volume 14, no. 93, 1969, pages 851–858.

"Paul Siple" (obituary). *Allegheny College Bulletin*, winter 1968–69, pages 3–4.

"Paul Siple: Authentic Hero" (editorial page). Meridien, Connecticut: *The Morning Record*, Nov. 30, 1968.

Peterson, Robert. "The Way It Was: With Byrd in Antarctica." *Scouting*, vol. 82, no. 5. (October 1994), pages 15–16.

Shaffer, Michelle. "90 Degrees South." *Allegheny Magazine*, 1989, vol. 9, no. 2, pages 2–6.

Siple, Paul. "My Four Trips to Antarctica." *The Book of Knowledge Annual*. New York: Grolier Society, 1948, pages 125–129.

Siple, Paul A. "Through Scouting I Found My Lifework." In 8-page pamphlet *Merit Badge Counseling,* National Association of United Methodist Scouters, Ministry of Scouting, no year and no page numbers given.

"Some Stars of *Boy's Life*." *Boy's Life*, March, 1986, page 3.

Yost, Edna. "Paul Allman Siple." *Modern Americans in Science and Technology*, pages 125–141.

Internet Sites

"Antarctica"
http://cia.gov/library/publications/the-world-factbook/geos/ay.html

Boy Scouts of America National Council: "Antarctica"
http://www.scouting.org (search Antarctica; Antarctic Scout Program information)

Byrd Polar Research Center Archival Program:
http://www.library.osu.edu/sites/archives/polar/flightexhibit/men.php

"Eagle Scout Siple with Admiral Byrd in the Antarctic"
www.scouting.milestones.btinternet.co.uk.siple.htm

"Facts About the US Antarctic Program"
http://www.nsf.gov/pubs/stis1994/nsf92134/nsf92134.txt

"Paul A. Siple: 1908–1968"
http://www.south-pole.com/p0000111.htm

"Paul Siple and the Origin of Windchill"
www.wemjournal.org/pdfserv/i1080–6032–010–03–0174.pdf

"Paul Siple: Man of Cold and Wind"
www.islandnet.com~see/weather/history/siple.htm

"Richard E. Byrd: 1888–1957"
http://www.south-pole/p0000107.htm

"Where is the Real South Pole Really?"
www.southpolestation.com/pole/survey.html

Persons Consulted

Ruth Siple (now deceased)
- Paul Siple's wife
- Past President of Antarctican Society
- Editor, *Antarctican Society Newsletter*
- Accompanied her to christen the *Laurence Gould* ice breaker
- Phone interviews and personal interviews

Jane Siple DeWitt
- Paul Siple's daughter
- Phone interviews, personal interviews, and e-mail interviews

Dr. Alton Lindsey (now deceased)
- Paul Siple's best friend
- Scientist on Byrd's 1933–35 Antarctic Expedition
- University professor
- Phone and mail interviews

Dr. Paul Dalrymple
- Past President of Antarctican Society
- Editor, *Antarctican Society Newsletter*
- Antarctic explorer, meteorologist
- Personal interviews and e-mail discussions

John Splettstoesser
- Past President of American Polar Society
- Past President of Antarctican Society
- Geologist at scientific research stations in Antarctica
- University professor, geology
- Lecturer for Antarctic tour groups
- Personal interviews and e-mail discussions

Dr. Richard Chappell
- Eagle Scout selected to go to the South Pole Station in 1957
- Served under Paul Siple, the Scientific Leader of the South Pole Station
- Professor, Biology
- Personal interviews and e-mail discussions

Antarctic Scouts Program:
Corresponded by e-mail and personal interviews with the following Eagle Scouts who went to Antarctica as part of this program:
- Dr. Richard Chappell
- Mark Leinmiller
- Benjamin Pope
- Louis Sugarman